FLATPACK:

READY-TO-GO
ASSEMBLY IDEAS
FOR 11-14s

© Scripture Union 2004
First published 2004

ISBN: 1 84427 099 8

Scripture Union, 207–209 Queensway, Bletchley, Milton Keynes, MK2 2EB, England
Email: info@scriptureunion.org.uk
Website: www.scriptureunion.org.uk

Scripture Union Australia, Locked Bag 2, Central Coast Business Centre, NSW 2252,
Australia
Website: www.scriptureunion.org.au

Scripture Union USA, PO Box 987, Valley Forge, PA 19482, USA
Website: www.scriptureunion.org

Scripture marked (NCV) quoted from The Youth Bible, New Century Version
(Anglicised Edition) © 1993 by Nelson Word Ltd, 501 Nelson Place, PO Box 141000,
Nashville, TN 37214-1000, USA

Scripture marked (NIV) from the HOLY BIBLE, NEW INTERNATIONAL VERSION.
© 1973, 1978, 1984 by International Bible Society. Anglicistion © 1979, 1984,
1989. Used by permission of Hodder & Stoughton Ltd.

British Library Cataloguing-in-Publication Data.
A catalogue record of this book is available from the British Library.

Printed and bound in Malta by Interprint.
Cover design by Wild Associates Ltd.

Scripture Union is an international Christian charity working with churches
in more than 130 countries, providing resources to bring the good news of
Jesus Christ to children, young people and families and to encourage them to
develop spiritually through the Bible and prayer.

As well as our network of volunteers, staff and associates who run holidays, church-
based events and school Christian groups, we produce a wide range of publications
and support those who use our resources through training programmes.

CONTENTS

BIBLE BASE INDEX

Old Testament

Genesis 1:26-31 Human beings are special (outline 15)

Genesis 1:27 Made in God's image (9,22)

Exodus 20:1-17 God's rules for our good (20)

Exodus 20:7 Don't use God's name thoughtlessly (1)

Exodus 20:16 No lying (2)

1 Samuel 16:7 It's what you're like on the inside that's important (7,9,12,14)

Psalm 139 God knows everyone and each person is special (14,15,18)

Proverbs 3:5 Depend on God (23)

Proverbs 10:18; 11:13; 16:28; 18:8; 26:20 The effects of gossip (6)

Proverbs 16:11 The importance of honesty (2)

Isaiah 53:4-6 Jesus' death in our place (21)

Amos 5:11,12; 8:5,6 Fairness (2)

Micah 6:8 Treating others right (4)

New Testament

Matthew 2:1-12 The Wise Men bring gifts for Jesus (33,34)

Matthew 5:9 Being a peace maker (8)

Matthew 5:13 Being like salt (27)

Matthew 5:9,38-48 Forgiveness and putting things right (31)

Matthew 12:33-37 What you say shows what you're really like (1)

Matthew 15:16-20 What makes people unclean (30)

Matthew 22:37-40 Loving God and others (20,26)

Matthew 28:20 Jesus promises to be with his followers always (17,24)

Mark 2:1-12 Friends are important because they support and help you (18)

Mark 8:31-38 Jesus talks about his death and resurrection (28)

Luke 10:25-37 The good Samaritan (11)

Luke 11:33-36 Light and darkness (30)

Luke 12:13-21 Being rich isn't what matters most (10)

Luke 18:18-30 Faith in God is more important than money (18)

Luke 18:27 Nothing is impossible with God (16)

Luke 19:1-10 Zacchaeus (14)

John 1:4,5; 9:5 Jesus is the light of the world (30)

John 3:16 God showed how much he loves us by giving his Son, Jesus (18,21,25,34)

John 8:32 The truth will set you free (3)

John 11:25,26 New life through Jesus (29)

John 14:6 The way, the truth, the life (3)

John 14:27 Jesus gives peace (8)

John 15:4,5 Jesus is the vine (17)

Romans 13:9 Loving your neighbour (4)

1 Corinthians 10:13 Coping with temptation (4)

1 Corinthians 11:23-26 A time to remember (32)

1 Corinthians 12:12-21 Working together, everyone matters (5,13)

1 Corinthians 13:4-13 Love (25,26)

Ephesians 2:10 Jesus was sent to help us (14)

Philippians 4:13 Jesus gives strength (17)

Colossians 3:10-15 Made in God's image (22)

Hebrews 13:8 Jesus never changes (19,24)

James 2:1-9 Treat people right, whatever they're like (9)

James 3:3-12 The power of the things we say (1,6)

1 Peter 2:24 Christ died for our wrongs (21)

CONTRIBUTORS AND ACKNOWLEDGEMENTS

All the outlines in this book have been contributed by those experienced in leading school assemblies. Contributors include Scripture Union staff and associates, teachers and others involved in schools ministry. SU Scotland and SU Northern Ireland also provided valuable ideas and suggestions.

We are grateful to Scripture Union staff worker, Ruth Wills, who was involved in the planning for this book and worked hard to persuade others to contribute their outlines. Ruth has also written the introduction to this resource and created some of the assembly ideas. Thanks, too, to Derek Goforth, for the ideas in outline 21, and Anne Jablonski for helpful suggestions and comments in the planning of this book.

We're also grateful to staff at Longbenton Community College for allowing us to include some of the outlines used in their Key Stage 3 assemblies.

Our thanks go to all the following for being willing to share their ideas and experience:

Andy Banks
Dave Bartram
Geoff Brown
Phil Brown
Liz Burgess
Tim Cutting
Wayne Dixon
Caroline Foreman

Andy Gray
Lis Greenbank
Dot Lee
Bruce Lockhart
Andrew Marshall
Keith Wills
Ruth Wills

About school assemblies

'Collective worship' – or 'assembly' – is a legal requirement of school life. It is a time in the day when all pupils have an opportunity to learn about God, have space and time to reflect and think, and to make an appropriate response. DfES guidelines say that collective worship should be 'wholly or mainly of a broadly Christian character' and should take place in school every day. This time provides an opportunity for Christian teachers and visitors to present something of the Christian message within a moral and holistic framework. It may challenge and stretch students' thinking about what they believe and as they consider life issues in the light of faith. It also gives an opportunity for Christian visitors leading assemblies to deliver a clear message about their faith, challenging misconceptions as students hear first-hand from a practising Christian believer.

The lives of young people aged between 11 and 14 are marked by change. They change from the security and familiarity of a primary school context to the wider and more daunting world of secondary school. Their bodies begin to change, as do their emotions, and their capacity to deal with certain situations. Their attitudes change, too, and the world around them can become a confusing place in which to live.

In Stages of Faith (Harper and Row, 1981), James Fowler writes about the years leading to and including puberty as a revolution: a revolution in emotional and physical life. He uses the mirror as a symbol. A mirror reflects bodily changes, but the metaphorical mirrors of culture, peers, media and family also provide the images that the early adolescent self then reflects. He comments that the young person needs friends and trusted others who will participate in

7

nurturing and developing the new feelings and insights that they will experience. The construction of personal identity and relationships are key at this age, and God can be identified as someone who cares, guides, supports and loves them. Adolescent thinking becomes more abstract and the capacity to ask big questions about God and life grows as the ability to reason with others and hold opinions develops further, providing teachers and volunteers with a great opportunity to encourage personal reflection and response. And, in your assembly, you can have fun! The activities in this book will provide you with entertaining and interactive ways of teaching and learning.

This assembly book is for Christian teachers and visitors alike. There are over thirty outlines for you to pick up and use or adapt as necessary. The easy-to-follow outlines make for straightforward preparation, as well as providing you with a range of issues and themes relevant to your students, each presented in a fun and enjoyable way. Every outline includes ideas to provoke further reflection on the assembly topic. The issues-based ideas in Section 1 address some of the concerns young people are facing in life. Teachers might want to follow these up in RE sessions or the ideas might fit into a PSHE/Citizenship programme. Other outlines deal with the matter of personal identity and how God can be relevant in their lives. The seasonal outlines in Section 4 make use of the opportunities which annual festivals present for talking about what Christians believe.

Each outline follows a uniform structure, but provides opportunities for flexibility. Teachers might like to use them as a starting point or to spark their own ideas for collective worship or classroom teaching. If you are a visitor, we hope that you will be able to use the book to select relevant outlines that offer you an opportunity to express something of your own personal beliefs. Teachers are incredibly busy people and many struggle to find time to prepare quality acts of worship. Drawing on visiting speakers gives an opportunity for members of churches or Christian groups to offer a valued service to their local school. A well as supporting and encouraging Christian teachers, a variety of visitors supply a broad view of the faith. On the whole, schools are extremely grateful to local people who are willing to help and support them in this way.

GUIDELINES FOR VISITORS

There are, however, some important points to bear in mind when leading a Key Stage 3 act of collective worship.

The government guidelines place an emphasis on Christianity as the major religion in the UK. They also give a special status to Jesus. However, some schools might have a special exemption called a 'determination'. This means that they have applied to become exempt from being 'broadly Christian' in nature. A partial determination may mean that young people worship in their own faith group. A whole determination may mean that the focus of worship is through a faith structure other than Christianity. Visitors to schools need to be aware of this when offering to conduct acts of worship. Some schools may also provide written guidelines for visitors to abide by. It is important that these are upheld, and that any policies for worship are read.

Things to remember...

- You are a guest in the school! You therefore should work within the school's guidelines and principles and not your own. It is useful to do some background work prior to your visit to familiarise yourself with the normal procedure for collective worship and to identify the mix of social and cultural backgrounds represented in one assembly. It is also good to know which faith groups are in attendance, and whether the school emphasises the Christian character of worship, or if it has a determination.

- School assemblies are usually quite short – they tend to be around ten minutes in length. This means that your assembly content needs to be clear, simple and to the point. Try to work around one teaching point and stay away from anything complicated or difficult to execute. Remember, less is more!

- As a visitor who is a practising Christian, you can be explicit about your faith. However, what you say should, as appropriate, be qualified as a statement of your own personal belief and not as something that the young people should believe themselves. You do not want them to compromise any faith or belief that they already hold. It is helpful to use the term 'Christians believe', indicating you are speaking about your own point of view.

- Collective worship is a time when the pupils can listen, learn, reflect and respond, but it is not a time for confessional activity.

- It is not a church! It may be appropriate to pray at some point and you might like to invite the young people to join with you, although not all will do so. But largely, singing is not a part of Key Stage 3 worship and usually is not something enjoyed by young people at this age!

Some warnings...

- Be careful not to use religious language or jargon in your presentation. A high proportion of the young people will not have the same church background as you and no assumption should be made as to any knowledge of the Bible, faith or Christian culture.

- Be careful not to tell the students what to believe. Instead, provide them with opportunities to think about what they do or don't believe.

- Be careful that you don't appear to have a hidden agenda. Some assemblies might have the obvious purpose of making or strengthening links with the local church, and maybe involve promoting an event. However, if this is not the agreed reason for your invitation to take an assembly, and teachers and pupils then perceive that what you do and say is merely an undercover advert for the local church or youth group, you may not be invited back – and you also may close any opportunities for other potential Christian visitors to that school.

  Schools appreciate an ongoing relationship, and your commitment to serving them will itself say something about your faith. It's a privilege to be allowed to work with a school to encourage the spiritual life of its students.

- Be careful not to overrun. In secondary schools, where lessons follow a strict timetable, an assembly which goes on too long will affect the whole school day. Some staff or pupils may need to get to the furthest extremities of the school buildings for the next session, so a punctual finish will help them greatly.

- Be careful not to embarrass any pupils. Although it is fun to have interactive and light-hearted activities in your presentation, it is inappropriate to put young people in a situation where they cannot make a useful contribution, or feel embarrassed about something they don't know or can't do. Additionally, don't use specific young people as examples to illustrate your point. Encourage and affirm at all times.

- Be careful not to overexcite the pupils. Normally, collective worship takes place early on in the school day. If the young people leave the assembly having been excited unnecessarily, the teachers will have a more difficult time trying to settle them down for the next session. A time of quiet at the end of your assembly gives an opportunity to reflect, respond – and calm down!

MAKING CONTACT WITH A SCHOOL

Initial contact with a school is normally made through a Christian teacher, member of staff or governor of the school.

The opportunity to take an assembly might arise from an invitation from the school because of the contact you have.

It might also come as a result of a developing relationship between members of a local church and staff at the school.

Your initial contact might be in the form of a letter to the head teacher or governors, followed up by a telephone call and a possible visit. The visit enables the visitor to introduce themself and find out about the ethos and distinctives of the school. A good starting point is to offer to make a presentation to the pupils at the time of a Christian festival such as Christmas or Easter. This would present you with an opportunity to communicate what Christians believe about the meaning of these special times.

Following your visit, it is important to continue the relationship by writing to thank the staff, and to offer your services for another time. Remember that your presentation and continuing relationship with the school will also communicate something about your faith to school members, staff and pupils alike.

Some tips

- Arrive early. Any problems with traffic can affect your arrival time, so leave with plenty of time. There will a major panic if the visitor arrives with only a minute to spare!

- Make sure you have everything you need. And also ensure that any electrical equipment such as an OHP or CD player are available and work!

- Dress smartly. Secondary schools often have quite a formal dress code. If you know staff at the school personally, you could check on what's appropriate. If you don't know the school, play safe – a jacket, at least, for men, and 'smart-yet-practical' for women.

- Keep to your allocated time. Overrunning is never popular with staff, neither is a long assembly with the young people!

- Be aware that, as teachers are very busy, they might not have much time to talk to you. But be assured that your efforts are worth it! You will be appreciated!

- Young people at Key Stage 3 are less responsive than those at primary school. Their body language and apparent lack of enthusiasm might initially be off-putting. However, they will enjoy your presentation more than they will be keen to let on!

- Make sure that you really enjoy the assembly yourself. Be confident in your message and approach.

How to use this book

All the outlines in this book use the same format. There is a balance between fun and more reflective elements. Stay focused on the aim and follow the outline – while making it your own – and you should be able to plan and lead a fun, challenging and balanced assembly. The preparation should not be onerous or time-consuming. However, careful and thoughtful planning is important. Being familiar with the outline, having the examples you need before the assembly begins, and memorising stories you're going to be using will all contribute to your success.

Your introduction might take the form of a game, demonstration or light-hearted activity. This will be related to your aim. It is wise to keep the aim in mind when planning and delivering the assembly. The gimmicks, illustrations and fun elements are simply tools for the introduction or reinforcement of your aim and the points you are trying to make. After the introductory section, you can then talk about the main point from a Christian perspective. This leads to a time of reflection and the opportunity for response that is usually done in a time of quiet. It may be appropriate for you to pray. Check beforehand that the school is comfortable with this happening.

If the school is a church school, there will generally be more of a commitment to a Christian message and ethos in the act of worship. Students may be accustomed to visits from the local vicar, curate, priest or lay workers. Such schools will expect and be used to a Christian message being clearly and confidently communicated and your visit has the benefit of enhancing the Christian experience of the students in the school.

Each outline is broken down into the following sections:

Bible base

Although the Bible verses suggested here may not actually be read in the assembly, it is important to keep in mind the Bible base as the starting point for the assembly content. It is helpful to go to the Bible passage at the start of your preparation, in order to ground what you plan to do in biblical teaching.

Aim

The aim shows what each assembly outline hopes to achieve. It also highlights what the young people will learn or take away with them. It is good to hold it in mind throughout the assembly, to provide a focus and keep you on the right track!

Tools needed

A well-planned and carefully thought through assembly is usually a good assembly. Some outlines require preparation that involves the locating of materials or equipment. This section provides a checklist of what you need to find in advance of the assembly.

Preparation

This section tells you about any particular preparation needed before taking the assembly. You might need to learn a 'script', prepare a quiz or devise a creative method of telling a story. You will also need to know the outline thoroughly without having to hold this book as you speak. It is important that you have rehearsed, read and thought about what you are going to say well in advance.

Presentation

This section provides a straightforward, step-by-step outline. It provides a skeleton of ideas in a logical sequence for you to follow. However, it is not a script. Every school and group of children is different, so it is important that you are aware of how appropriate the activities are for your group. The flexibility offered in each outline provides you with the opportunity to fine tune your presentation, using your own words and style and being sensitive to the personality of the school.

Reflection

This section is where the link is made between your presentation and the aim. This is the opportunity for you to ask questions and talk about the meaning you have tried to communicate through the presentation. In this section, there is the opportunity to encourage the young people to reflect on how God is relevant to aspects of their lives considered in the presentation. This section will require thought and preparation and prayer, as you consider what you want to teach and the students to learn, and how you will do this in a sensitive way which is also appropriate to the school context.

Response

This is the opportunity for the young people to make a response to what has been said. Keep in mind the question, 'So what?' Some outlines will suggest using the 'Response' section as an opportunity for prayer, some will suggest a time of silence, and others provide a question to reflect on. It might just be a time of silence. It is this section that aims particularly to move the young people on in their spiritual development.

Each part of the outline is important to consider. There is room for flexibility and for the ideas in each outline to kick-start your own. Please use his book as a starting point for your own creativity, but also do keep in mind the above points in order to present a clear, cohesive and engaging act of collective worship.

Whether you're a visitor to school or a teacher – whatever your own experience of Christian faith, or the kind of school or students you are working in or with – we hope you will find this book a great resource as you put together assemblies for 11 to 14s which help them grow in their thinking about life, faith and God.

1 Tongue twister

Bible base	Exodus 20:7; Matthew 12:33–37; James 3:3–12
Aim	To help students think about the things they say, and reflect on how these can help or hurt others.
Tools needed	❏ Two or three 'tongue twisters'. ❏ Display equipment (large pieces of card, OHP and acetates or PowerPoint and projector). ❏ Blindfolds (two or three will be enough). ❏ A few different foodstuffs for a taste test. Include contrasting foods: salty, sour, sweet – things the students will like and things they won't. Avoid any to which people may have common allergies. ❏ Suitable containers and spoons.

PREPARATION

• Write out your tongue twisters for display on OHP acetates, card or PowerPoint.

• Put the chosen foods into the containers and make sure you have as many spoons as you have volunteers.

PRESENTATION

1 Start with all or some of these interactive ideas to introduce the theme of the tongue and what you say.

Tongue twisters

Get everyone saying one of the tongue twisters you have written up. Let them do it with the words on display at first, then without. If you have the words written on separate pieces of card, you could remove a few words at a time. Depending on the time available and enthusiasm of students, do one or two different ones.

Tongue-tied

Ask the students if any of them can curl their tongues. Can anyone touch their nose with their tongue?

Tongue-taster

Ask for two or three volunteers. Blindfold the students and ask them to taste some food (check first that your volunteers do not have dietary food allergies, eg nuts). Let the audience, but not the volunteers, know what's being tasted. Ask your volunteers to guess what each foodstuff is.

2 Follow this up by pointing out how important the tongue is for talking. Ask students to think about the things they say.

- Do their words help others or hurt them?
- How much of what they say is positive and encouraging?
- Do they often swear or say negative things?
- Are they rude to others?

Ask them to think about the kind of words they use in their everyday speech, for example: in the last couple of days have they said words which have hurt or encouraged someone else? Have they been rude to anyone, or sworn at someone?

REFLECTION

Say that you are going to read some things about the importance of the words we use from the Bible. Use a contemporary version, for example CEV or NCV (the Youth Bible).

• Read James 3:3–12. Comment on the passage, giving some examples of how a few words can cause enormous problems. The students might have some examples of their own. Emphasise how we can let good and bad words come out of our mouths. These verses suggest that the words we say have something to do with the kind of people we are on the inside (verse 12).

• Read Exodus 20:7. How do you use God's name? As a swear word? The Ten Commandments talk about not misusing God's name. Even if you don't believe in God, remember that lots of people do. When you use God's name in this way you might be offending others.

RESPONSE

1 Ask students to think about how they speak to people. Is it good and positive? Or unkind and often putting others down?

2 There's the suggestion in the Bible verses that thinking about God – what he's like, how he wants us to live – will make a difference to the kind of people we are on the inside. For example, what's your thought life like? Are there ways in which you need to change on the inside?

3 Decide to do something positive about the words you use today. You could try today:

• not to swear;
• not to use God's name as a swear word;
• to say something positive and encouraging to at least one person.

4 Encourage students to ask God to help them do what they've decided.

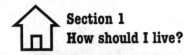
| 2 | # Honestly! |

Bible base	Exodus 20:16; Amos 5:11,12; Amos 8:5,6; Proverbs 16:11
Aim	To help students think about speaking and acting honestly.

PREPARATION

• Make up four or five statements about yourself or the world – some which aren't true and some which are. For example:

'When I was younger, I released a CD which made the Top 40.'

• Think of some situations, relevant to the school you'll be visiting, where it might be difficult to tell the truth, for example because you don't want to hurt someone's feelings or get into trouble.

PRESENTATION

1 Tell the students that you are going to make a series of statements to them. They must vote on each one according to whether they think you are telling the truth or a lie.

Read out each of the statements you have prepared. After each, allow a few moments for students to decide whether what you've said is true or not. Then ask them to vote by putting up their hand for either option.

2 Tell the students which statements were true and which were false. Ask what helped them decide when you were lying and when you were telling the truth.

3 Ask the students the following, getting some feedback each time:

• On a scale of 1–10 (10 being very honest) how honest are you?
• Is it ever right to lie?
• What about 'little white lies'?

4 Give these examples of when they might not tell the absolute truth:

• Someone asks, 'Do you like my new haircut?' You think it's awful, but what do you say?
• Someone asks, 'Do I look thinner?' They don't! What do you say?
• You haven't done your homework, due today. What will you say to your teacher? The truth or a lie?
• You scratch a friend's CD. Do you tell them the truth or lie?

Add more, trying to make them relevant to your audience.

5 Ask what the honest thing to do would be in each of these situations. Is it always wrong not to tell the whole truth?

REFLECTION

Say that Christians believe they should be totally honest in all they do, because God is honest. Dishonesty usually leads to more lies and causes injustice, hurt and more dishonesty: for every lie you tell, you need another to cover up. It's better to tell the truth in the first place.

RESPONSE

Ask the students to think about the times when they have lied or not been honest and others have been hurt as a result. Give them the opportunity to say sorry to God for anything they have been dishonest about. Invite them to ask God to help them be more honest in all they do.

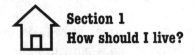
3 The truth is...

Bible base	John 8:32; John 14:6
Aim	To encourage students to think about what 'truth' means, whether they are always truthful, and why Jesus said that he is 'truth'.
Tools needed	❏ Statements for the 'True or False?' quiz.
	❏ For the game of Call my Bluff: a 'word' written out for display on a large piece of paper, OHP acetate or PowerPoint; three definitions written on cards, one of which is correct (choose a word that the young people are extremely unlikely to have heard before, and that, preferably, sounds funny).
	❏ Flip chart or OHP, acetates and pens (optional).

PREPARATION
• Prepare what you'll need for the 'True or False?' quiz and the game of Call my Bluff.

PRESENTATION

1 Start by telling the students that you are going to read out some statements and they must decide whether they are 'true' or 'false'.

Use your list of statements prepared beforehand. You could include factual statements which are definitely either true or false, and also include some which are to do with beliefs, opinions and values, in order to encourage discussion, for example:

- The acceleration due to gravity is 9.81 m/s on Earth. (True)
- Mozart wrote 'Twinkle twinkle little star'. (True)
- The Battle of Hastings took place in 1066. (True)
- Life exists on other planets.
- I love my parents.
- The sun rises in the east.
- God exists.
- Smoking is bad for your health.
- The Bible is true.

Talk about some of their answers. Ask them what criteria they used to decide if the statement was true or false.

2 Play a version of the TV quiz game, Call my Bluff.

- Display the 'word'.

- Ask for three volunteers to come to the front who think they can convincingly say what the word means. Give each person one of the 'definition' cards. Only one person has the card with the correct meaning; the other two 'meanings' are incorrect.

- Get each of the volunteers to read their card, then to tell the audience what the word means as convincingly as they can.

- When the three volunteers have finished, ask the audience to vote on which they think is the true meaning.

- Now, reveal the 'true' one. Again, ask the question: 'What criteria did you use to decide if what you were being told was true or false?'

REFLECTION

1 Ask: 'So, what is truth?' Get the students to come up with some definitions. Depending on time, you could ask for a volunteer to write up some of the suggestions on a flip chart or OHP for everyone to see.

2 Read out the two Bible passages (John 8:32 and John 14:6). Ask the students some open-ended questions about the passages, for example:

• The Bible speaks of Jesus as being 'the truth'. What do you think that means?
• What is meant by 'the truth will set you free'? What 'truth' was Jesus talking about?

Note: Be careful how you speak about these verses, remembering that there may well be faith groups other than Christian present in the assembly. Where appropriate, use the phrase, 'Christians believe that…'.

3 Can students think of some ways in which knowing or telling the truth about things makes them 'free', and examples of how being lied to, or not knowing the truth, can hurt people or make them confused?

RESPONSE

In a time of quiet:

• Invite the students to think of a time recently when they have not been altogether truthful. Invite them to say sorry to God for their actions and thoughts.

• Say that one of the reasons Christians believe that the truth sets us free is because we can be forgiven through Jesus for all we've done wrong, including not always being truthful.

• Read out John 8:32:

> **'You will know the truth, and the truth will make you free.'**
> John 8:32 (NCV)

4	**Peer pressure**

Bible base	Micah 6:8; Romans 13:9; 1 Corinthians 10:13
Aim	To help students think about whether they resist peer pressure or go along with whatever others are doing.
Tools needed	❑ A selection of football shirts, including two or three from the most popular teams in your area and one from the least popular team.

PRESENTATION

1 Ask for volunteers who support the teams you have shirts for to come forward to represent their team and put the appropriate shirt on. Ask for another volunteer to put on the unpopular team's shirt.

2 Try to persuade your volunteers to change their alliance to the less popular team and wear that shirt instead. You could use arguments like:

'You'll look cool if you wear this.'
'Only idiots wear United tops. Put this on instead.'
'I'll give you a prize if you wear this shirt.'
'Everyone else is wearing one like this!'

Add any other arguments/tactics you can think of to persuade them.

Unless you have some very weak-willed volunteers, your volunteers will probably prefer to keep the shirt they already have instead of accepting the less popular shirt.

3 Point out how stupid your arguments were for persuading people to wear the less popular shirt.

REFLECTION

1 Point out that if they are unwilling to change the team they support just because someone thinks the shirt looks stupid, it makes even less sense to change the kind of person they are, the way they behave or what they believe, just because others tease them, for example, for being loyal, working hard, being kind to other people.

2 Ask for some examples of when it might be difficult to stand up for what you think is right, and not give in to pressure from others (eg pressure from others to lie, mess about in class, be unkind to others).

3 Say that it can be difficult sometimes to know what is right. Point out that Christians believe God has given us guidelines, for example:

'Love your neighbour as you love yourself.'
Romans 13:9 (NCV)

4 Encourage students not to give in to peer pressure, or be afraid to stand up for what they think is right. Say that Christians believe God will help them not to give in to pressure to do what's wrong (1 Corinthians 10:13).

RESPONSE

1 Ask the students to think of some examples when they find it difficult to know what's right or to do the right thing in school or at home.

2 In a time of quiet, ask them to decide now to do what's right today even when it's hard, or when it would be easier to go along with the crowd. If they like, they could use this time to ask God to help them.

5 Working together

Bible base	1 Corinthians 12:12–21
Aim	To help students understand that people are stronger when they work together and support each other.
Tools needed	❑ A telephone directory.

PRESENTATION

1 Invite to the front three or four volunteers who think they are strong. Challenge them, one by one, to rip the telephone directory in half in less than five seconds. Tell them that the first one to do it will win £10.

2 After all three have tried – and failed – ask them why they couldn't do it. Tear out the first page or two and ask them if that will help.

3 Say that you want them to do some maths. Tell them how many pages there are in the directory. Tell them that they have to divide this number by the approximate number of people there are in the room. Ask for their guesses about the number, but give them a definite approximate number for the calculation. Agree on the answer.

4 Tear out this number of pages. (Check beforehand that your answer is not likely to be more than ten.) Give the ripped-out pages to one of the volunteers and ask them to see if they can tear these into two (point out that your offer of a £10 prize no longer applies!). Have your volunteer rip the pages, which this time they should be able to do.

5 Tear out two more lots of the same number of pages from the directory. Give these to the other two volunteers. On a given signal ask them to rip their pages in two.

6 Encourage applause for the strength of your volunteers and ask them to sit down.

7 Point out that even though it's hard to rip up a whole directory on your own, it's easy if the directory is divided up amongst lots of people who work together. In fact, if there was time in the assembly, you could have given everyone a few of the pages and then together you would have been able to have ripped the telephone directory in two in under five seconds. As a group of people working together, you are much stronger than when you work on your own.

REFLECTION

1 Talk briefly about how everyone has a part to play – we can't do everything ourselves. We all need to help each other. What is impossible for one person alone isn't so difficult for a group working together. There's a description in the Bible of the church (ie a community of Christians) likening it to a body. Everyone's gifts and talents are needed just like hands and toes are all important for a body. Everyone is important.

Whether or not we're Christians we're all part of different communities (eg family, school) where we have a special part to play. We need to work together with others and help them too as they do their part.

2 Working together makes sense whatever you believe, but Christians believe that what really makes a difference is remembering to rely on God because he is the one who really helps us to achieve the impossible.

RESPONSE

In a time of quiet, ask the students to think about:

• If there are projects you are working on with others, how good a part of the team are you?

• Who could you help today?

Conclude by encouraging them to pray, asking God to give them the strength and confidence to be able to do this.

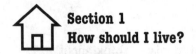

6   I say, I say

Bible base	James 3:3–12; Proverbs 10:18; 11:13; 16:28; 18:8; 26:20
Aim	To encourage students to think about the things they say and the effect these have on others.
Tools needed	❑ A list of sayings for the quiz. ❑ Bible verses from the outline (optional). ❑ Display equipment, eg large piece of card, OHP and acetates or PowerPoint and projector (optional).

PREPARATION
• Write the Bible verses selected for use in the assembly on OHP acetates, card or prepared on PowerPoint slides.

PRESENTATION
1 Explain that this assembly is all about the kind of things we say.

2 Begin with this quiz to start people thinking about the subject. To add interest, you could divide your audience in half and see which side gets most correct. There are some examples below for the

quiz. Add more, or different ones, depending on current films and TV programmes that you think the young people will be familiar with.

Ask your audience who said the following well-known sayings, which are all from films:

'Life is like a box of chocolates.' (Forest Gump)
'May the force be with you.' (Star Wars)
'We wants it we does, my lovely, my precious.' (Lord of the Rings)
'Shaken not stirred.' (James Bond)
'Hacuna matata.' (Lion King)
'To infinity and beyond!' (Toy Story)

3 Ask the students to think for a moment what the world would be like if we took the things people say literally, for example:

'I'll murder you if..'
'I never want to see you again.'
'Pigs might fly.'
'Get lost.'

4 You could ask them to suggest some more examples. Comment/speculate on what the consequences could be if we all took such examples literally.

5 Comment that, sadly, the words we use, whether or not they are meant to be taken literally, are often destructive and negative. They can hurt other people. Ask them to think about, but not say aloud, when they did or said one of the following in the last 24 hours. Read the list slowly, giving time for reflection:

• lies
• gossip
• quarrelling
• nasty comments
• angry words
• exaggeration
• slander, about other people
• insults, to someone's face

All these kinds of words hurt others.

6 Tell the students that the Bible has got quite a lot to say about the kind of words we use to others. Say that you're going to read some which are all about gossiping, something we're probably all guilty of. You could simply read from the Bible, or have these displayed on OHP as you read:

> **'Anyone who spreads gossip is a fool.'**
>
> Proverbs 10:18 (NCV)

> **'Gossips can't keep secrets, but a trustworthy person can keep a secret.'**
>
> Proverbs 11:13 (NCV)

> **'... and a gossip ruins friendships.'**
>
> Proverbs 16:28 (NCV)

> **'The words of a gossip are like tasty bits of food. People like to take them all up.'**
>
> Proverbs 18:8 (NCV)

> **'Without wood, a fire goes out; without gossip, quarrelling stops.'**
>
> Proverbs 26:20 (NCV)

> **'A big forest fire can be started with only a little flame. And the tongue is like a fire.'**
>
> James 3:5,6 (NCV)

REFLECTION

1 Comment that words can help people, as well as hurt them. Ask them to think of ways in which what they say could encourage others, make others feel happier, or help others.

2 Ask the students:

• What kind of words will come out of your mouth today?
• Will you say mainly positive or negative words?

RESPONSE

1 Allow a short time of quiet and ask the students to think about how they speak to others.

2 Challenge them to decide:

• not to gossip about others today;
• to say at least three positive things to other people today, for example something to encourage, a compliment, an apology to someone they know they have hurt with unkind words.

3 If they like, they could ask God to help them do these things; they could say sorry for bad things they've said; and ask God to help them watch their words so that others are helped, not hurt.

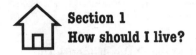

7	**Strength test**

Bible base	1 Samuel 16:7
Aim	To help students understand that 'strength' is not just about physical strength, but also about having the strength inside yourself to do what is right.
Tools needed	❏ Three balloons, one of which needs to be a giant balloon. ❏ A container or box with a pretend spider (or a real one!). ❏ A simple brain-teaser or riddle (see example below).

PREPARATION
• Before the assembly begins, set up a table or other suitable surface and two chairs where the audience will be able to see for the arm-wrestling contest.

• Find and write up on a large piece of card a brainteaser or riddle, for example, the sequence: O T T F F S S ? (What are the next two letters in the sequence? Answer: 'E' and 'N'. The letters are the first letter of the numbers 1 to 9 written as words, so 'E' and 'N' represent Eight and Nine.)

PRESENTATION

1 Start by getting students to think about strength with illustrations from current news or TV programmes that they will be familiar with (eg World's Strongest Man).

2 Explain to students that in this assembly you're going to be finding out how strong some of them are. Ask for three volunteers to take part in a series of strength tests – two boys and one girl works well.

Arm-wrestling

Have an arm-wrestling contest with each volunteer. Set this up so that everyone in the audience can see the contest. Make sure you lose at least one round. Talk about the physical strength needed to arm wrestle.

Balloon race

Next, give each of your three volunteers a balloon. Give the giant one to the person who beat you in the arm-wrestling contest. Tell the contestants that the first one to blow up their balloon and burst it by blowing it up (no nails or pins!) is the winner.

Get the other students to cheer the competitors. Whether or not anyone manages the balloon challenge, when you've ended the contest, comment that this test needed physical strength (keeping on blowing into the balloon), but also courage – no one likes the idea of a balloon bursting in their face!

The spider test

Introduce your pretend (or real) spider! Are the 'tough' arm-wrestlers so brave now? Is being 'tough' always about being fearless? Sometimes even the biggest, 'toughest' people are afraid of creepy crawlies!

Note: Keep this light-hearted, being careful not to make any of your volunteers feel embarrassed.

The brain-teaser test

Show the brain-teaser to your contestants (and audience). Can the contestants work it out? (No help allowed from the audience.) Their physical strength or bravery can't necessarily help them now; a different kind of strength is needed to get the answer and succeed. Tell everyone the answer to the brain-teaser if no one can work it out.

3 Thank your contestants and ask them to return to their places.

REFLECTION

1 Comment that all kinds of strength are needed in life: physical, mental and academic strengths all have a part to play in life.

2 Ask how 'strong' they think they are when it comes to making some of the big decisions in life about right and wrong. Point out that it often takes strength to do what you know or believe is right (give some examples which you think are relevant to your audience).

3 Ask how they know what is right and wrong. Explain that everyone needs to have a basis for decisions about moral or ethical issues. Explain it has to do with:

• Character: what you are like (eg honest/dishonest, reliable/ unreliable, fair/unjust etc).
• Values: what's important to you (eg you only think about yourself; you're concerned about others).

Both of these have to do with what you're like on the 'inside' – not how physically strong or how clever you are.

4 Briefly refer to the story in the Bible about the choice of David as king in 1 Samuel 16. David was chosen not because he was a good-looking singer who fought wild animals, but because of the strength of character and the person he was, which God saw on the 'inside' (1 Samuel 16:7).

RESPONSE

1 In a short time of quiet, ask the students to reflect on:

• What do you think your strengths are (eg sport, dancing, music)?
• What do you think are your strengths of character (eg working hard, being a good friend)?

• What are your values (eg right, wrong, honesty, morals)?
• Do you need to change anything or do something differently?

2 Ask the students how they might need to be strong in standing up for what's right. Conclude by challenging them to be strong enough to make good choices and to decide to make a difference in good ways today.

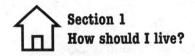

8 Peace makers

Bible base	Matthew 5:9; John 14:27
Aim	To help students think about what Jesus said about peace and what they can do to work for peace in their own situations.
Tools needed	❏ Clipboards and pens. ❏ Small prizes for each of your volunteers (small chocolate bars etc).

PRESENTATION

1 Tell the students that you are going to play Blankety Blank (like the TV quiz show), teachers versus students.

Note: If it isn't appropriate to ask teachers to be involved, have two groups of students competing against each other instead, for example boys versus girls.

Ask for three volunteers for each 'team' (or select team members).

2 Give both teams a clipboard and pen. Tell the students that you are going to read out a phrase and they must write on their clipboard what they think should go in the blank. Round one is for student one, round two for student two etc.

Round one

The phrase for student one is 'Happy _____'. (Answers might include: birthday, Christmas, New Year, Easter, anniversary, hour, go-lucky.)

When the student has written their answer, ask your teacher team to consult together and decide what they think the student has written, then write their answer down.

Now, get the student to show what they've written. Then, ask the teachers to show what they've put. Did the teachers get it right? Award them a point if they did.

Talk about the word 'happy'. Say that everyone likes feeling happy! It usually means everything is going well for us. It's been said that 'happiness' is about 'happenings'. If what happens to us is good, we are happy; when bad things happen to us, we are not!

Round two

The phrase for student two is 'War _____'. (Answers might include: correspondent, head, dance, lord, time, crime, cry, paint, memorial.)

As for round one, when the student has written their answer, get the teachers to write down what they think the student has written. Get them to show their answers and award the teachers a point if they get it right.

Talk about the word 'war'. Comment that there is a lot of conflict in the world today, not just between countries. There are all kinds of conflict between different groups of people: different communities, neighbours, family members, even friends. When conflict happens, it brings lots of unhappiness to many people. The opposite of war is peace.

Round three

The phrase for student three is 'Peace _____'. As before, ask your student volunteer to write their answer. (Answers might include: talks, maker, pipe, time, offering, treaty.) Then continue as for rounds one and two.

Talk about the word 'peace'. Peace is a great thing if you have it or can get it. Peace is the opposite to war. It also can mean the absence of noise. And, it can be to do with the way we are feeling on the inside, meaning an absence of turmoil, anger, unrest, panic and unhappiness.

6 How well did the teachers do at guessing what the students wrote? Give small prizes to the winning 'team' (or to all your volunteers!). Thank your volunteers and ask them to sit down again.

REFLECTION

1 Ask the students to think about peace for a few moments:

• Would you say you have got peace in your life?

2 Tell the students that you are going to read some words from the Bible that Jesus said about peace:

> **'Those who bring peace are happy,**
> **because God will call them his children!'**
> Matthew 5:9 (NCV)

3 Comment that peacekeepers are people who keep the peace whatever the cost! Peace makers are people who make peace where there is trouble and disagreement.

4 Ask students to think about:

• Are you a peacekeeper, or a peace maker?

RESPONSE

1 Get everyone to close their eyes. Spend some time in silence. Enjoy the peace, the tranquillity and absence of noise.

2 Ask them to think about what needs to happen for there to be peace in the world, in situations where they know there is conflict. What needs to happen for them to have peace in their own lives? Say that Christians believe that God gives peace.

3 Now ask students to think about how they could help to bring 'peace on earth' in the different situations which they are involved in.

4 As your conclusion, say that you are going to read some more words from the Bible which Jesus said to his disciples when they were frightened and worried. Encourage students to remember anything which is troubling them at the moment and then to imagine that Jesus is saying these words to them:

> **'I leave you peace; my peace I give you. I
> do not give it to you as the world does.
> So don't let your hearts be troubled or
> afraid.'**
>
> John 14:27 (NCV)

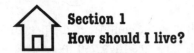

**Section 1
How should I live?**

| 9 | **What's your image?** |

Bible base	Genesis 1:27; 1 Samuel 16:7; James 2:1-9
Aim	To help students think about image and understand that, whatever your image, you are special and valuable.
Tools needed	❑ OHP, pens and acetates or a flip chart. ❑ Selection of teen magazines.

PREPARATION
• Before the assembly, check that it's possible to use an OHP and that all the equipment works.

PRESENTATION
1 Ask students to think about examples of some of the following:

• a typical business person
• a typical footballer
• a typical TV celebrity
• a typical young person

Include different examples which you think are relevant to your particular audience, but make sure the last example is the typical young person.

2 Ask a volunteer to come to the front and draw a quick sketch of their idea of one of the typical characters you've mentioned (leave the 'young person' until last), either on an OHP acetate or on a flip chart. Talk about the sketch, then ask for another volunteer to draw another 'typical' example. Finally, ask for a volunteer to draw a typical young person.

3 As each drawing is finished, talk about it, asking students for their ideas about what they would expect people like that to wear, or how they would expect them to behave, for example:

• What does the typical footballer/young person wear?
• How do they speak?
• How do they behave?
• What do they do?

4 Talk about the 'typical' young person, encouraging students to give some ideas on how typical young people look or behave. There will probably be some difference of opinion!

5 Make the point that when it comes to how we look and live, all of us are searching for identity and acceptance by others: our culture seems to put lots of emphasis on body image. Give some examples from current teen magazines (eg Bliss, Cosmo Girl), TV programmes or celebrities. Comment that people worry about how they look, being too thin, too fat, too spotty or too tall etc.

6 Give some examples of how the pressure to 'look good' has caused illnesses for some people, like bulimia, anorexia and depression. Some people get bullied because they haven't got the 'right' image.

REFLECTION

1 Ask the students to think about their image, encouraging reflection and feedback with questions like:

- What kind of image do you project to others?
- Is it the real you?
- What do others think of you?
- What do you think of yourself?
- How do you think God sees you?

2 Say that Christians believe God has made people in his own image, and that he loves each person for themself and has made them special, whatever they look like. Comment that this means we can know we're OK – you don't have to have some other 'right' image. It also means we need to accept others, whatever they're like, and treat them with respect and care.

3 If it's appropriate, read these Bible verses: 1 Samuel 16:7; James 2:2–4,8.

RESPONSE

1 Ask students to think about their own image. Is this a true reflection of what they are really like, or is it a mask?

2 Ask them how they think God sees them, as he looks at their thoughts and attitudes to others.

3 Remind them that Christians believe that whatever they are like – tall, short, thin, fat, spotty, super-model, clever, sporty or not – God loves them and thinks they're special. Created by God, that's the only 'image' that's important.

10 Who wants to be a millionaire?

Bible base	Luke 12:13-21
Aim	To help students reflect on whether it makes sense to want material wealth for its own sake.
Tools needed	❑ Sweets for prizes, enough for at least three or four 'rounds' of the game, eg one tube of Smarties, a Mars Bar, a small box of chocolates, a big box of chocolates. ❑ Three or four questions, each with a choice of four answers for the 'Who wants to be a "chocolataire"?' game.

PREPARATION

• Prepare your questions and the choice of answers for each. Think about what the school and students you will be visiting are like. You could include questions relevant to that particular school. Include some answer options which are just for fun. Don't make the quiz too easy, but use questions and answers which will make it likely for your volunteer to 'win'.

PRESENTATION

1 Start by asking how happy they are with what they are like, and with what they own. Say that you are going to have a vote. You want them to put up their hands for each of the following.

Hands up if...

• you would like to be better at sport.
• you think you are pretty good at sport already.
• you would like to be better at art.
• you would like to be a better singer.
• you would like more money.

Comment briefly on their voting, pointing out that on the whole people would like to be better at things than they are at present, even things they are quite good at anyway.

2 Ask: 'Who wants to be a millionaire?' Mention the TV game show, briefly making it clear what the game is about, in case some of the audience haven't seen it. Say that you're going to play a version of this now called, 'Who wants to be a "chocolataire"?'

Ask for a volunteer who would like to be a 'chocolataire'. Play the game with increasingly 'difficult' questions, but with answers likely to be known by this age group. Include some entertaining ones too. They must choose between four answers (a, b, c, d) and can use the lifelines of: 'Ask the audience', 'Phone (ask) a friend', and '50/50'. Award the increasingly bigger prizes after each round (ie Smarties, a Mars Bar etc). Aim to get your volunteer to the last prize!

In your role of the game show host, build up the tension with appropriate commentary and comments to the contestant and the audience.

Note: Adjust number of rounds and time you take to play this, according to the amount of time you have for the assembly. Be careful not to let this go on for too long.

REFLECTION

1 After your 'winner' has been congratulated and thanked, comment that Who wants to be a millionaire? is a great programme, it's very entertaining etc. Then point out that, although it's enjoyable to watch, the game plays on people's greedy nature: to get more, even though they've got plenty; the feeling that more is better; the desire to get what you want.

2 Tell the Bible story of the farmer who kept building bigger barns (Luke 12:13–21). Explain that through the story Jesus makes the point that this man was foolish for spending his whole life worrying about getting wealthy, when he wasn't going to be able to keep it anyway. As far as God was concerned, he was poor, not rich, because he only cared about himself.

RESPONSE

1 Explain that Christians believe God has given us the responsibility of using what he has given to us – our possessions, talents and abilities – wisely for him, for the good of others.

2 In a time of quiet, ask students to think about these questions:

• How do I use what I have?
• How do I use my money?
• How do I use my gifts, abilities and talents?

3 Challenge the students to try to give something or use one of their talents for someone else today.

4 If appropriate, end with a short prayer, thanking God for all he has given us, and asking for his help to use the gifts he has given us for the good of others.

5 You could finish with a comment that, while there's no pressure, the 'chocolataire' might like to share their fortune after the assembly!

Note: Check with the school first, that they are happy for chocolates to be given out in this way, and that encouraging the winner to share his prize isn't likely to cause problems for teaching staff or others.

| 11 | **Respect!** |

Bible base	Luke 10:25–37
Aim	To encourage students to value and care for one another, whatever their differences.

PREPARATION

• Spend some time rehearsing your reading of the 'newspaper article', which is made-up and based on the story of the good Samaritan. Decide whether you can adjust the story or add current/local interest details to make it more appropriate for the particular assembly you will be leading.

PRESENTATION

1 Tell everyone that you are going to make three statements. Ask them to put their hands up if they agree with the statements. Hands down between each statement.

a) I am the most important person here.
b) I like it when people listen to me.
c) There has been a time in my life when I have been treated unfairly.

Respond as appropriate to your audience's reaction to the three statements.

2 Talk about the three ideas:

a) Tell them that they are looking at the most important person here – YOU! Make sure they know that you are joking. Go on to qualify the statement, saying that before they think you are a complete big-head, each of them is also the most important person here. Each of them is also sitting next to the most important person here. Give any other examples appropriate to the situation. Comment that we all have great value because God made us. And to appreciate others, we need to value ourselves.

b) Say that if we like it when people listen to us, we should listen to others. Ask, 'How much time do you spend actually listening to others and putting others first?'

c) Ask everyone to think about whether they always treat others fairly. Be honest. Ask, 'How do you treat others, especially people you don't get on with?'

3 Tell the students you are going to read them the following extract from a newspaper article. Add current/local details to add interest. Read the 'article'.

Police overwhelmed as thugs go on rampage!

By our law and order correspondent

Police were outnumbered yesterday as thugs went on the rampage. Officer Peter Smith was patrolling near to the riot when a gang of youths attacked and mugged him, 'leaving him for dead', as a colleague later put it.

Though no one appears to have witnessed the attack, it is reported that several passers-by walked straight past the injured officer and some even turned and walked the other way to avoid getting involved.

The surprising twist in this story is that Ian Thomson, the notorious football hooligan wanted by the police, stopped and helped the man. Not only did he administer first aid, but he then took the injured man to a private hospital where he paid for all the bills. He was indeed a 'good Samaritan'.

4 Tell the students that, in fact, this 'article' was made up. Explain that it is an updated version of the story in the Bible about the good Samaritan. Jesus was talking to his fellow Jews, who hated the Samaritans.

5 If appropriate and if there's time, you could also read the story from a contemporary version of the Bible: Luke 10:25–37.

REFLECTION

1 Comment that the story in the Bible makes it clear that people (including those who are different from us) are equally valuable and that we should treat others with care and respect. Jesus told this story to illustrate what it means to keep one of God's commandments in the Bible:

> **'Love the Lord your God with all your heart, all your soul, all your strength and all your mind … Love your neighbour as you love yourself.'**
>
> Luke 10:27 (NCV).

2 Challenge the students to think about how they treat others – including those who aren't their friends or whom they don't like.

RESPONSE

1 Ask the students to think about one or two others in school whom they consider 'different' from themselves, or whom they don't value. Now ask them to think how they could show they value them or times when they could be 'a good Samaritan' to those people.

2 Encourage everyone to be quiet for a few moments to think about this, and decide to do something about it today. If appropriate, you could suggest that people might like to ask God's help to do this.

12 Inside out

Bible base	1 Samuel 16:7
Aim	To encourage students not to judge others by outward appearance, but to think about and value what they are like on the 'inside'.
Tools needed	❑ Four or five CD covers (choose current CDs with different music styles, eg pop, rock, heavy metal, jazz). ❑ Empty crisp packet. ❑ £5 note. ❑ Four or five full crisp packets.

PREPARATION

• Fold up the £5 note and stick it lightly into a corner of the empty crisp packet, so it can't be seen by the audience, or fall out.

PRESENTATION

1 Show the students a variety of CD album covers. For each cover you show, ask them to say the name of the band and the album title. Ask who likes each one.

2 Ask for suggestions about the kind of people you think might like, for example, the pop album and the heavy metal album. Comment that we often make assumptions about the kind of people who like different types of music. Point out that, in fact, people often aren't anything like how we expect them to be because of their taste in music.

3 Now show the crisp packets and ask the young people which crisp packet they would prefer: the empty packet (say, 'I ate them!'), or one of the full ones?

4 Choose someone who wants the full packet. Ask why. Give out the packets of crisps. (Tell them to save them for break time!)

5 Hold up the 'empty' crisp packet. Ask why they think people weren't so keen to have the empty packet. Talk about what makes them think it's not worth having.

6 Now extract the folded £5 note from the 'empty' packet. Make the point that although the packet looks 'rubbish', inside there's something valuable.

REFLECTION

1 Explain that often we judge people and things by what they seem like on the outside. Then we make all kinds of judgements about what we think they must be like on the inside.

2 Briefly outline the story of David being chosen to be king. Read 1 Samuel 16:7. Comment on how his family didn't think he was very special because he was the youngest and just looked after the animals. But God saw he was special and had great plans for him.

RESPONSE

1 Ask the young people to think about whether they judge others because of the way they seem on the outside, for example: how they look, the music or clothes they like.

2 Remind them that God understands what people are like on the inside – and that's more important than just looking good.

3 Pray, or allow a time of quiet with the opportunity for students to think or pray silently:

• Ask them to think of one or two people in their class whom they don't know very well, and to think of at least one good thing they've noticed about them which is not to do with outward appearance, music tastes etc.

• Ask for God's help in looking beyond someone's outward appearance.

• Thank God that he knows what we're like on the inside and values each of us for who we are.

Note: The first section of the outline about CDs could be omitted for shorter assemblies.

13 Everyone matters

Bible base	1 Corinthians 12:12–21
Aim	To help students learn that each person is needed and important.
Tools needed	❏ A current, popular CD (make sure lyrics are appropriate for use in a school context). ❏ Equipment for playing the CD. ❏ A large picture of a compact disc.

PREPARATION

• Before the assembly, set up and test equipment for playing the CD track. Check that you are at the right point on the CD for the track you plan to use.

PRESENTATION

1 Start by playing an extract from a track on the CD.

2 Encourage a response to the CD:

• Do students like this band/performer?
• Do they like the CD?
• Do they own this album?
• What CDs do they like at the moment?

3 Comment that now CDs aren't just used for music. Get responses from the students about all the things CD or DVD technology can be used for (eg music CDs, discs for computer and DVD).

4 Hold up/put on display the large picture of a compact disc (optional). Give some information about CDs, for example:

• CD information is recorded information.

• It's not the CD itself you listen to, but the disc contains information that is 'read' by a computer or CD player. The information tells the computer or CD player what sounds to make.

• A CD stores the information in patterns in a long spiral.

• The information is held in 'binary', which means the signals which make the sounds are either on or off. This tells the computer in the CD/DVD player what sounds to make and how loud to make them.

5 Ask for six to eight volunteers. Ask them to stand in a straight line. Point out how each person is a different size. Comment that on a CD there are many pieces of information of many different sizes.

6 Ask them to imagine what would happen if some of the information on the CD were not there (remove three students from the middle of the line). Ask for their suggestions, then point out that the missing sections of information would mean that your film would have a blank bit, or there would be a gap in your music. Every bit of information, however big or small, is important on a CD.

REFLECTION

1 Comment that every person in the assembly has value, a part to play, in their school. It doesn't matter how small or new they might be! And it doesn't make you more important if you are taller, stronger or more clever than other people. Each person is unique. Without you, something would be missing – a bit like music on a CD being spoilt if there was information missing from the disk.

2 In the Bible, Christians are described as being part of 'the body of Christ'. Read 1 Corinthians 12:14–21. Explain that this picture emphasises that everyone has a different role to play, and each is as important as another. Without any one individual, something important would be missing.

RESPONSE

1 Ask students to think about what skills and gifts they have that do, or could, contribute to school life.

2 Pray, or allow a time of quiet, encouraging people to:

- thank God for making each person unique and important;
- pray that he will help them recognise their skills and use them wisely.

Note: If appropriate, you could play some more of the track from the CD that you used at the beginning of the assembly as the students leave.

14   What are you worth?

Bible base	Psalm 139:13,15; 1 Samuel 16:7; Ephesians 2:10; Luke 19:1–10
Aim	To help students consider that each one of them is valuable to God.
Tools needed	❑ Ten cards with one name each of people who are currently media celebrities (pop, sporting and political celebrities), for example:
	Ronaldo Victoria Beckham Tony Blair George W Bush Sir Paul McCartney Sir Elton John Mohammed Al Fayed Sven Goran Eriksson Bono Richard Whiteley
	❑ Current pop video/DVD, video/DVD player and TV.

PREPARATION

• Prepare the cards.

• Before the assembly, set up equipment to show the pop video and make sure it's ready to start.

PRESENTATION

1 Ask for ten volunteers and give each one a card. Give them one minute to arrange themselves into the order of what they think each character is worth – the most valuable on the left and least valuable on the right.

Encourage some response from your audience. Do they agree with this order? Would they say some of the characters are worth more or less?

Ask your volunteers to go back to their places.

2 Now give your audience the following choices, allowing some response after each. You might want to substitute other examples which are more current or appropriate to your audience.

Would you rather have:

• Prada/Next/George at Asda?
• Holiday in Bahamas/holiday in Spain/holiday in Bognor?
• Friends like Brad Pitt/Busted/Pauline Fowler?
• Four-bedroomed house in Surrey/semi in Bolton/one-bedroomed flat in Toxteth?
• Satellite TV, all channels/5 channels on a portable/flickering black and white?
• Champagne/Bucks fizz/Tizer
• Mercedes SLK/5-door Fiat Punto/B reg Volvo with rust?

Note: Adapt the examples here to suit the area and school you are in.

3 Watch a pop video by a current and popular band or artist. Ask the students:

• Why do we want to be like these people?
• What qualities do they have?

REFLECTION

1 Say that Christians believe the good news is that God loves us all, whatever we're like. He is not impressed by things like wealth, beauty, fame or talent. He is interested in what we are like on the inside.

2 Briefly tell the story of Zacchaeus (Luke 19:1–10). Comment that Jesus loved Zacchaeus (the cheating tax collector) for who he was, not for what he had or hadn't done. This is a picture of how he loves us too. Christians believe that God created us and we are unique, and he places a high value on all of us. He has a purpose for each person here, even though that might not including getting a number one single in the charts!

RESPONSE

Encourage the young people to close their eyes as you read the following verses:

• Psalm 139:13,15
• 1 Samuel 16:7
• Ephesians 2:10

Give the opportunity for response in a time of quiet, encouraging the young people to think about what they mean to God, and what plans he might have for them in the future.

15 You're amazing!

Bible base	Psalm 139; Genesis 1:26–31
Aim	To encourage students to appreciate the 'specialness' of themselves and one another.
Tools needed	❏ Additional 'amazing facts' about the human body (optional).
	❏ OHP, acetates and pens.
	❏ Ink/paint pad – washable (optional).
	❏ Damp wipes for cleaning up.
	❏ Mirror in picture-style frame.

PREPARATION
• You could make a simple paint pad by soaking poster paint into kitchen towel, placed on a paper plate. Test to find out what works for best results on an OHP acetate before the day of the assembly.

• Make sure OHP equipment is available and is set up ready for your assembly.

PRESENTATION

1 Did you know? Tell your audience these amazing facts about the human body (substitute or add others if you like):

- Your brain is more complex than the most powerful computer.
- When you read, light falls on 14 million colour sensors and 200 million black and white sensors, sending countless electrical impulses along the optic nerve to the brain.
- Your heart beats around 100,000 times in one day (36,500,000 a year).
- Your lungs inhale over 2 million litres of air every year.
- You give birth to 100 billion red blood cells every day.
- Your skin is constantly renewing itself.
- You have about 60,000 miles of blood vessels.

2 Talk about some of the ways in which every person in the room is unique, for example:

Your signature

Ask for one or two volunteers to come and write their signature on OHP acetate, then display it. Comment that our signatures are all different. They are often used as proof of identity. However, some people are so good at forging signatures, it's difficult to tell the difference from the real thing. Here are some other ways in which you are unique, where you can't fool other people.

Your teeth

Comment that forensic scientists often identify bodies by their unique set of teeth.

Your eyes

Encourage everyone to look into the eyes of the person sitting next to them and notice what's special about them. Comment that they are all looking at something amazing. The uniqueness of the human eye can be used for security: a camera can be programmed to recognise your unique eye pattern and so unlock a door for you.

Your fingerprints
Ask for one or two volunteers to come to the front and, after pressing their fingers on a pad of paint or ink, make some fingerprints on an OHP acetate. Point out how each fingerprint is different from the others. Encourage everyone to look at their own fingerprints. Comment that their uniqueness means that they can be used in crime detection – your fingerprints could link a crime to you! Give the example of a burglar who tried to destroy his fingerprints by putting his fingers in acid, but was later convicted when the skin grew back in the same unique fingerprint pattern!

Your DNA
Explain that your whole body has a unique DNA pattern which is frequently used for solving crimes.

3 Comment that it's not just your physical appearance that is unique. We're unique in all kinds of ways. Illustrate this by taking a vote on some of the following:

• Tell a short joke. Who thought it was funny? Who didn't?
• Talk about a current pop group. Who does/doesn't like them?
• Discuss your favourite/least favourite food. Who does/doesn't like it?
• Who is a fan of your favourite football team?
• Talk about a TV show you do/do not like. Who does/doesn't like it?

Comment that your tastes are unique. You are also unique in how you feel, how you think and how you respond to things which happen to you. There is no one like you and no one like me. There never has been and never will be.

4 Disguise a mirror, so that from the back it looks like a picture frame. Say that you have a picture of a really special person. Ask for a volunteer to come and have a look, to see if they agree. Tell them that they mustn't comment on what they see, only answer your question.

Ask them to walk around your 'picture frame' to look, so that the audience don't see that it is a mirror. Of course, when your volunteer looks, they see a 'picture' of themselves. Ask your volunteer: 'Is this a really special person?'

Repeat this with two or three volunteers, then turn the 'picture' around so that everyone can see that the 'picture' is really a mirror.

REFLECTION

1 Comment that Christians believe God created men and women 'in his image' and said that this bit of his creation was 'very good'. You could read here some or all of Genesis 1:26–31.

2 Comment that everyone is special – in the entire world there is no one else who has been, or is, like you.

3 Say that Christians believe God has got a plan and a purpose for everyone, and has given them the special gifts and talents needed for that. Ask them to think about what their unique role in God's world might be.

RESPOND

In a time of quiet, encourage students to:

• Thank God for the person he has made them to be, and for the special-ness of their family and friends.

• Think, or pray, about how they might use their special talents at this stage of their lives, and in the future.

Notes: To shorten the outline: omit some of the examples of how the body is unique (eg signature, DNA); or don't take votes on the personal taste issues in section 3, just talk about these.

Make sure that paint or ink used for the paint pad is washable.

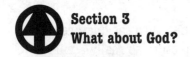

16	**Nothing's impossible!**

Bible base	Luke 18:27
Aim	To explain that Christians believe God can help you with 'impossible' situations.
Tools needed	❑ Several pieces of paper, all different sizes (eg A3, A4, A5). ❑ Jelly in a bowl and chopsticks (enough for each volunteer in Challenge 2). ❑ Aprons (one for each volunteer in Challenge 2). ❑ Towel.

PREPARATION
• Before the assembly, get ready for Challenge 2. Make sure there's a suitable table available; position it ready for use; put the jelly in the bowls etc.

• Check that the school is happy with you doing a messy activity and make sure the floor is protected if necessary.

PRESENTATION

Ask for three volunteers, ready for a challenge.

Challenge 1

• Tell your volunteers that you are going to give them each a different-sized piece of paper. The challenge is to fold over a piece of paper eight times.

• Give out the different-sized pieces of paper and ask them to get folding. The volunteer with the biggest piece of paper may think that their task is easier, but in fact it isn't. Everyone will find that it is impossible.

• Allow a few moments for everyone to try to complete the task, providing a commentary on their progress for the audience. Once it's clear that it's not so easy as it looks, stop the challenge and thank your volunteers.

Challenge 2

• Ask for another three volunteers, telling them that they have a different challenge.

• The challenge is to eat jelly with chopsticks! Quickly set up three bowls of jelly with chopsticks for each on a table, facing the audience.

• Provide your volunteers with aprons. Who can finish their jelly first? The volunteers will find that it is almost impossible and very messy!

• Provide a commentary for the audience, and stop the contest after a few moments.

REFLECTION

1 Comment that folding the paper was more difficult than you might expect, and eating jelly with chopsticks was impossible!

2 There are lots of things in life that seem difficult or impossible too (eg maths homework). Sometimes we face big decisions, we're going through a bad time in a relationship, or just not coping with work.

3 The Bible says that with God nothing is impossible. This doesn't mean that everything is going to be easy. But, Christians believe, it does mean that he is bigger than every problem or difficult situation. At this point, you could read Jesus' words in Luke 18:27.

4 You may like to give some personal examples of when God has helped you with an 'impossible' situation in your life.

RESPONSE

1 Say that Christians believe we can tell God about the difficult situations in our lives and he will help us with them.

2 Ask the students to close their eyes and reflect on any difficult situations in their lives.

3 Now ask them to imagine God – bigger than the universe, the world, our country and their problem! Invite them to give their 'impossible' situation to him now – and watch out for what happens!

Note: Clear up any mess afterwards!

17   Going solo

Bible base	John 15:4,5: Philippians 4:13; Matthew 28:20
Aim	To help students think about our need to rely on others and God. Others might let you down, but, Christians believe, you can always rely on God.
Tools needed	❏ A sock puppet (or a real puppet if you have one). ❏ A suitable table.

PREPARATION:

• Make a simple puppet, if you haven't got one. This can be very simple, for example: use a long (so it goes up your arm) sock, add 'eyes' (paper, or plastic ones from craft shops).

• Practise with your puppet! Rehearse your conversation with him until you can do it without forgetting your 'lines'.

Notes: The first part of this assembly is 'led' by you and the puppet. Remember the age group of your audience. Make sure that they know you are not serious about this, and don't expect them to take it seriously either. Overplay your role as puppeteer, exaggerating the way you talk to the puppet. Don't worry about any 'mistakes' – make them entertaining.

Give your puppet a name and always call it that name. However unconvincing your puppet looks, if you appear to believe in him, your audience will join in the game of suspending their disbelief! Stay 'in character' from the beginning of the assembly until you make plans for your world tour!

PRESENTATION

1 Introduce yourself and your puppet.

2 Then hold the following 'conversation' with the puppet. This outline is a guide for your own improvisation. Use your own words:

Leader: Say to the audience what a good team you and [puppet's name] make. You rely on each other for everything and are going to take the 'puppet world' by storm!

Puppet: Shakes his head.

Leader: Ask [puppet's name] what the matter is.

Puppet: Whispers in your ear.

Leader: Say to the audience that [puppet's name] said he is 'going solo'. He wants a career of his own, as you are holding him back.

Puppet: Whispers in your ear again.

Leader: Tell the audience that he says you are not good-looking enough! Pretend to be really upset. Tell [puppet's name] that he needs you in order to be a funny puppet. Without you, he can't be funny.

Puppet: Whispers to you again.

Leader: Explain that [puppet's name] says he is terminating his contract and is leaving you... right now!

Wipe a tear from your eye, say how much you will miss him etc. Then take your hand out of the puppet and lie him on the table. Pause for a moment as if waiting for him to sing, speak etc. Nothing happens. Act as if trying to encourage some movement, but still nothing happens. Encourage the audience to shout, pantomime fashion, to the puppet to move.

Of course, nothing happens. You put your hand in the puppet and he comes back to life again!

The puppet: Whispers to you.

Leader: What?

The puppet: Whispers in your ear again until you finally 'understand' what he is saying.

Leader: Tell the audience that [puppet's name] said that he's realised he can't do anything without you.

Tell [puppet's name], and the audience, that he's absolutely right. Begin to make plans for your world tour!

3 Pause – and make it clear that you are now coming out of your character as puppeteer.

REFLECTION

1 Comment that often we think we can look after ourselves and don't need other people. We don't listen to those around us, we don't follow advice, we try to get what we want and do as we like. Point out that it doesn't work (give some everyday examples from life at home or school). We all need others.

2 Say Christians believe that everyone needs help to live life, to make right choices, to help them cope with all the things that happen. Explain that, just like your hand in the puppet gave it life, so Christians believe that Jesus gives them 'life' – God is always with them, willing to help them.

Other people sometimes let us down, but Jesus has promised to be with everyone who relies on him (see Matthew 28:20). Christians believe that God will guide you and help you. Sometimes, when we try to live without him and 'go solo', we end up in a real mess (see John 15:4,5). The Bible also says that we can do all things with the strength he gives us (see Philippians 4:13).

RESPONSE

1 In a time of quiet:

  • Encourage the students to reflect on whether they are trying to live life without thinking about or relying on others.

• Say Christians believe that God wants to be involved in our lives, helping us and showing us how to live. We can't live our lives to the full without him ('But without me, they can do nothing.' John 15:5, NCV). Comment that everyone has a decision to make about this, either to let God be in their life or to go it alone.

• Invite people, if they would like, to tell God about anything that's bothering them or they need help with today.

2 Finish by encouraging them to remember the words of Philippians 4:13.

'I can do all things through Christ, because he gives me strength.'
Philippians 4:13 (NCV)

18 What's most important?

Bible base	Psalm 139; Mark 2:1–12; Luke 18:18–30; John 3:16
Aim	To encourage students to think about what's most important to them in life, to consider whether God is important to them and whether faith in God makes a difference to how they live.
Tools needed	❏ OHP, acetates and pen (optional). ❏ The theme tune to Friends (by the Rembrandts). ❏ A recording of the Bros song 'When will I be famous?' (optional). ❏ Brief extracts from a recent or current TV reality show and Who wants to be a millionaire? (optional). ❏ Equipment to play the above in the assembly (optional). ❏ Football shirt, hat, scarf (optional). ❏ Ready-prepared acetates, cards or PowerPoint slides with quotes about faith from Jonathan Edwards and others etc (optional).

PREPARATION:

• Prepare the extracts from songs or TV shows which you're planning to use in the assembly and make sure that you have all the equipment you need, or that it is available from school.

• If possible, set up and test the equipment in the room where the assembly will take place before the students arrive.

• Prepare visuals with quotes about faith, if using.

PRESENTATION

1 Begin by asking students what's most important to them/to people generally? Get some suggestions from students. If you have an OHP, write up their suggestions so everyone can see them.

2 Point out that the things we feel are most important in life are the things which most affect the way we live and behave.

3 Comment that if you asked each person in the room, everyone would say that different things are most important to them. Say that you're going to talk about some suggestions which lots of people might put as their top things for being important. They all happen to begin with the same letter (which could help them remember and think about them later).

Talk about each of the things below (omit some of the suggestions if time is short).

If you think your audience is comfortable to do so, you could begin your discussion of each of the following by asking people to put up their hands to show how important they think each one is.

Family

Ask, 'How important to you is your family?' Say that families are very important to us. We are all part of a family, although sometimes our families are not easy to live with. Ask for some suggestions of why that might be (be sensitive, as some young people present might have difficult family circumstances). You could keep the tone light and general, by briefly giving some personal, funny anecdotes of things you've found difficult in your own family (eg a prank one of your older siblings played on you!).

Make the point that, although they can be places of worry, frustration and concern, our families are very important to us and have a huge influence on the way we live and the kind of people we are.

Friends

If possible, introduce this by playing a brief extract from the theme tune to Friends. Ask the students to guess from this what your next most important thing is for people. Again, ask them how many of them think that 'friends' are one of the most important things in their lives.

Draw attention to the words, 'I'll be there for you!' in the song. Friends matter. Some people make friends when they first start school and remain friends for the rest of their time at school – even for the rest of their lives. That's great!

You could mention briefly here the Bible story in Mark 2:1-12 where four friends brought a paralysed man to Jesus for healing. His life was changed because of the support of his friends.

Remember that some people feel very lonely in school, so this might be a difficult issue for them. You could acknowledge this in what you say, and encourage those lucky enough to have loads of friends to be aware of those who are on their own.

Fame

Ask, 'Do you want to be famous?' For some people, fame matters. Introduce this theme. If possible, you could play a short extract from the Bros hit song (a well-known band from a few years ago), 'When will I be famous?'. Or play a short clip from a reality TV show, eg Pop Idol.

Get response from the students about why fame is so important for some people. If it's not easy to show or play some examples on the theme, ask students for suggestions of pop bands which seem particularly concerned about fame; or ask about TV reality shows and why people want to take part in these.

Flatpack

Fortune

Ask the students who watches *Who wants to be a millionaire?*. Give any examples that you've watched recently, for example the competitor who was two questions away from a million, guessed wrong and 'lost' a lot of money! Talk about why money is so important to people.

You could briefly mention here the story in Luke 18:18–30 where Jesus told a very rich young man to give away all his money if he wanted real life.

Football

If you support a football team (you could pretend!), show the students something which will help them guess which team you support. You could introduce this theme by simply putting on your favourite football team's shirt (or scarf, hat etc) and asking them to guess what the next 'most important' thing is, then asking if they know which team you support.

Get some suggestions from the students of their favourite teams.

If possible, give a personal example to demonstrate how much football means to you. For example, crying when 'your team' lost an FA Cup Final!

Ask people for suggestions of why football matters so much to some people.

Faith

If possible, display these examples which show how important faith is to some people:

> **'I'm not defined by being an Olympic Champion but by God's love for me and mine for him.'**
>
> Jonathan Edwards

> **'Yes, I believe in God.'**
>
> Cassie Bernall, student at
> Columbine High School, Colorado, USA

Use these examples to introduce the idea that faith is very important to some people, although it may not be talked about or thought about much. Comment that faith – who and what you believe in – is very important. It affects the way we think about ourselves, other people and the way we behave.

Illustrate this by referring to any examples you have shown on OHP acetate, or simply quote and talk about them.

• Jonathan Edwards, for all his success (he has been the World Champion and the World Record holder for the Triple Jump), said the words in the quote after he won his gold medal in the Sydney Olympics. He believes his value doesn't depend on what he has achieved, but on God's love for him. His faith in God is what's most important, whatever else he's achieved.

• Cassie, a high school student in the US, believed her faith in God was more important than anything. When she was asked by a gunman if she believed in God, she is said to have give this reply, even though it led to her losing her life.

REFLECTION

1 Point out that, unlike Jonathan Edwards, you're not an Olympic Champion. Although you could mention in a self-deprecating way some 'important' sporting achievements of your childhood or youth (eg 'I once came third in the Bean Bag race at my school sports meeting). Then say that you are like Jonathan Edwards in one way: it is your Christian faith which matters most to you.

2 Explain that it's not just that God is important to you, but that you are important to God. Christians believe that all people are important to God.

3 Explain that Christians believe God showed how important and special we are to him by giving for us what was most important for him. Talk briefly about Jesus and the reason for his coming, death and resurrection.

4 Conclude by saying that whatever is important in their lives, God thinks they are important. Challenge them by asking how important they think God is in their lives and what difference faith in him might make to the way they live.

RESPONSE

1 In a few moments of quiet, ask the students to think about what's important to them. Mention, pausing between each, the five things you thought about first:

- Family
- Friends
- Fame
- Fortune
- Football

2 Now ask them how important faith in God is for them. Ask them to carry on thinking through today about things they might do differently if they acted as though God were most important.

3 Finish by reminding them that Christians believe God values them for who they are, whatever their successes or failures. They are special to him. You could read here: John 3:16.

Notes: The length of this outline is flexible. Check how much time there is for the assembly and make sure that you are not too ambitious in the amount of material you aim to include. If you think that this outline will be too long, you could omit 'fame' or 'football' from the examples of what is most important to people.

This outline includes elements which are particularly important and relevant for the age group: worth, identity, value, relationships with family and friends, the big questions of life (eg faith and God). In any adaptations you make try to retain the emphases on the age-related issues.

19 Always there for you

Bible base	Hebrews 13:8
Aim	To encourage young people to reflect on the Christian belief that whatever happens, you can trust God not to change.
Tools needed	❏ A music compilation CD and information from newspapers, all from the same year. ❏ CD player. ❏ Three juggling balls, each a different colour. ❏ Ability to juggle (preferable, but not essential!).

PREPARATION
• Find out the information you need (the Internet is a good source) and get appropriate old newspapers for the 'Name that Year' quiz.

• Practise juggling!

Note: If you can't really juggle, pretend you can! Be self-deprecating and laugh at your failures. Or, find a volunteer who can juggle and is willing to help you with this part of the assembly.

PRESENTATION

1 Begin with the quiz: 'Name that Year'. Choose three volunteers who are willing to play 'Name that year'. They are going to be given four clues for a particular year in the last decade:

- A music track from a CD.
- A newspaper headline.
- The title of a popular TV programme.
- The football team which won the Premiership in that year.

As soon as they know the answer, tell them to call it out, without waiting for the other clues.

Play a music track, read a newspaper headline, describe a popular TV programme and say which team won the Premiership, all in one particular year from the last decade.

Play three rounds with clues for three different years. Keep track of which of your volunteers gets the most correct answers. If you like, give a small prize to the winner.

2 Comment that, even in a short space of time like a decade, things change. Refer to a verse in the Bible, Hebrews 13:8, which says, 'Jesus Christ is the same yesterday, today, and for ever.' (NCV). Explain Christians believe that while life around us might change, God is always there for us.

3 Bring out the three juggling balls, each a different colour. Whatever your skill level at juggling, use this positively to engage with your audience, for example: start juggling and impress or look as if you know what you're doing, then fail. Keep this visual introduction to the next stage of the assembly brief!

Say that you are going to use the juggling balls to illustrate the idea of God being the same, yesterday, today and for ever – like you've read in the Bible verse. Juggle the balls and throw one over the top. (Do this as well as you can, but if you make a mistake just carry on with the next part of the assembly outline). Stop juggling and show the ball (colour one) you threw over the top. Say that this represents 'Yesterday'. Talk about how some people, particularly older ones, think a lot about their yesterdays. For example, they remember the 'good old days' when you could go to a football match, get the bus there and back, buy a bag of chips and still have change from a pound!

Juggle again and throw another ball over the top. Stop juggling and say that this ball (colour two) represents 'Today'. Comment that some people think only about today. They concentrate on what they can get now, because you don't know what will happen to tomorrow. It can make you greedy and selfish if you live for today only and want everything now.

Juggle again and throw the final ball over the top. Again, stop juggling, then say that this ball (colour three) represents 'For ever'. Ask what they think 'for ever' means. Say that 'for ever' maybe too long to get our minds around, so what about the future? Are they thinking about what will happen to them tomorrow, next week, next year, later in life – even, for ever?

REFLECTION

Pick up and refer to the three juggling balls as you encourage reflection on the Bible verse that says Jesus is the same yesterday, today and for ever. Say that Christians believe this means that God knows and understands all about our lives and is with us.

Our yesterdays

He understands what things have hurt us in the past. He also knows about the things we have done in the past which we shouldn't have done. He knows about our good times too. God will forgive us for the past and help us get on with today.

Today

He is with us today, in everything we do. Christians believe God loves us and wants to be part of our 'today' – and every day.

For ever

Christians believe that God will be with us in the future too. 'Eternal life' means being with God for ever, both now for all of our lives here on earth, and then after our lives here come to an end.

RESPONSE

1 In a time of quiet, encourage students to respond to what they have heard. Encourage them to think about their idea of yesterday, today and for ever. Invite them to think about God and respond in some of these ways:

• perhaps they need to accept forgiveness or forgive;
• maybe they would like to give their 'today' to God;
• maybe they can bring some future worry to him.

2 You could finish by reading the words from Hebrews 13:8 again.

20 It's good for you!

Bible base	Exodus 20:1–17; Matthew 22:37–40
Aim	To help students consider that following God's rules for life is a good way to live.
Tools needed	❑ Blindfold. ❑ OHP and acetate or PowerPoint and projector. ❑ Two or three balls of plasticine. ❑ Equipment for a simple obstacle course.

PREPARATION

• Before the assembly, arrange an 'obstacle course'.

• Write the words of Matthew 22:37,39 on an acetate or PowerPoint slide and set up the equpiment.

• Think of two or three suggestions for rules for plasticine 'people' to live by, which would be for their own good.

PRESENTATION

1 Ask for a volunteer to be blindfolded. Ask another student to guide the blindfolded student around your simple obstacle course (you could just go around the room if you don't want to use an obstacle course).

Tell the guide that they are only allowed to use words/instructions/ commands and must not touch the blindfolded person. When your volunteers have completed the course, thank them and ask them to sit down.

2 Ask the audience if they can remember what commands the blindfolded person was given by the guide.

• Why were they giving those commands?
• Who was benefiting from those instructions?
• What was the point of the instructions given?

Make the point that the instructions were given to help the blindfolded person get around the course in the safest and best way, and also to protect them from harming themselves.

3 Ask for two or three more volunteers to come to the front. Give them some plasticine and challenge them each to make a model person from it. Once the models have been made and admired, ask them to invent some rules that the plasticine people have to live by, rules that are especially for the good of plasticine people (eg keep away from fire or you'll melt). Ask the audience for suggestions and have some more of your own ready.

Ask your model-makers how they would feel if their plasticine person refused to do as they were asked and, for example, walked straight into a fire! Point out that not only might they feel rejected, it would be very stupid of the plasticine people to ignore the rules their creators had given for their safety.

REFLECTION

1 Comment that rules we have to live by are usually meant for our good. You could give some examples of school rules relevant to the particular school where you are leading this assembly.

2 Say that Christians believe God created human beings and gave us rules to live by which we can read in the Bible. The best known are

The Ten Commandments. Ask the young people if they can remember some. Talk briefly about two or three.

3 Explain that Christians believe God gave us rules, not to stop us from having fun, but to protect us and to provide us with a way of living together that's the very best for us. Illustrate this with some examples from the commandments you've mentioned (eg not stealing, not lying).

4 Tell them that Jesus said that The Ten Commandments could be summed up like this:

> **'Love the Lord your God with all your heart, all your soul and all your mind ... Love your neighbour as you love yourself.'**
> Matthew 22:37,39 (NCV)

Emphasise that God's rules are for our good and are meant to help us care for one another and to live together. When people go against the rules, others get hurt.

RESPOND

1 Ask the students to think about how they would feel if their plasticine person ignored their commands. Now ask them to think about how God feels when we ignore his rules.

2 Encourage them to think about whether they need to say sorry for any wrong things they've done and for the hurt that may have caused other people.

3 Suggest they might like to focus on Jesus' words about caring for others. How could they keep that 'commandment' and care for others today?

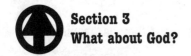
21	**Forgiven**

Bible base	Isaiah 53:4–6; John 3:16; 1 Peter 2:24
Aim	To help students understand more about the meaning of Jesus' death and why Christians believe it's important.
Tools needed	❑ Questions for a quiz. ❑ Shaving foam and paper plates. ❑ An assistant (could be a teacher). ❑ A towel. ❑ Three 'prizes' (eg Mars bars).

PREPARATION

• Make up three foam 'pies'.

• Before the assembly, prime and rehearse with your assistant.

PRESENTATION

1 Ask for three volunteers from your audience to take part in a quiz.

2 Explain the rules: if they answer all three questions correctly they will win a prize, but if they get any of the questions wrong there will be a forfeit.

3 Ask easy questions for the first two rounds. Then ask a question in the third round which will be too hard for them to answer, for example:

- Who won the FA Cup in 1914? (Burnley)
- How many bones in the hand? (At least 27)

4 When all the volunteers have answered their questions and got one wrong, then remind them that they knew the rules when they started this game, which said that if they got one of the answers wrong there would be a forfeit!

5 Bring out three shaving foam pies – one for each of your volunteers. At the last moment, before you put the pie into the face of the first volunteer, have your long-suffering assistant hurry to the front and plead for leniency.

6 Explain that what you are about to do is fair because the rules were clear and your volunteers got the answers wrong. The assistant offers to take the punishment in the place of the student. Repeat this for each volunteer – giving them the prize they don't deserve as they go to sit down.

Note: Your assistant will need a towel ready to wipe his face between each 'pie'!

REFLECTION

1 Use the above as an illustration of what Christians believe about why Jesus died. As appropriate to the particular school, and the understanding of Christian faith you think your audience may have, talk about: the rules God gave people to help them in their lives; the fact that people have chosen to do wrong; how Jesus took the punishment for our wrongs when he died; the promise of forgiveness.

2 Ask for 'hands up' to show if anyone thinks they have never done anything wrong. If any student does put their hand up, gently suggest that maybe they aren't telling the truth – so they have now!

3 Say that we all get things wrong each day – make sure you include yourself in this. We think wrong things, we say wrong things and we do wrong things. We've all failed to live the way God has shown us.

4 Say that Christians believe that, because Jesus took our punishment (which he didn't deserve), we can be forgiven and God won't hold against us whatever we've done wrong. Add that this doesn't mean we can do whatever we want: forgiveness involves our wanting to put things right and trying not to make that mistake again.

 RESPONSE

1 In a few moments of quiet, ask the students to think about:

- a time when they did/said/thought something wrong;
- a time when someone did something amazing for them.

2 Invite students, if they want to, to tell God about anything they know they've done wrong and to say sorry. Thank him for forgiveness.

3 To conclude the time of quiet, you could simply read one of the Bible verses or passage given in the Bible base at the beginning of this outline.

Note: Clear up any spills from the 'pies' afterwards.

22 Who are you like?

Bible base	Genesis 1:27; Colossians 3:10–15
Aim	To help students think about the Bible teaching that we are all made in the image of God.
Tools needed	❏ A card for the drawing task instructions. ❏ Three sheets of flip chart paper or similar. ❏ Three thick, black felt-tip pens. ❏ Blu-Tack (or similar).

PREPARATION

• Before the assembly begins, arrange your meeting room so that there is an area where your volunteers can do their 'portraits' without being observed by the other students (eg a space at the back, or to the side, or behind screens). Set up this area with the flip chart paper and felt-tip pens.

• Prepare a card with instructions for the drawing activity, as follows:

a) Get into pairs.
b) Decide who is going to draw and who is to be drawn.
c) Do your drawing, filling up the whole of the paper, so that everyone in the audience will be able to see it.

• Check with the teacher responsible for the assembly that this will be possible and ask if a teacher can, discreetly, supervise the students as they do their drawings.

PRESENTATION

1 Begin by inviting six volunteers to the front.

2 Tell the audience that you are going to ask your volunteers to do some drawing. Ask the volunteers to go to the pre-arranged part of the room where their work won't be seen by the other students. Tell them that they will find there the instructions and equipment they'll need for their drawing. Give them a short time limit (eg three minutes).

3 Whilst your volunteers are doing their drawings, do the following with the other students:

• Talk to them about times when relatives comment on how like their mum, dad, sister etc they are. Ask them about who they are like in their families. Comment that we can be like our relatives in the way we behave and in our personalities as well as our looks.

• Explain what your volunteers are doing: drawing three portraits. The audience are going to have to guess who each drawing is like, and who the 'artist' is.

4 Be strict about your volunteers keeping to the time limit, but encourage them to finish their drawings. Then ask them to come back to the front. Ask the adult who accompanied the volunteers to bring their drawings in. (It's important that the students can't work out who did each drawing by who is carrying which picture.)

5 Have the six volunteers stand in a line, not in their pairs. Then, one at a time, display each of the pictures. Ask the students who they think each picture is a drawing of. Once they have all been matched up, see if the audience can then match up the artists with their drawing. Surprisingly, no matter how badly drawn the pictures might be, they are usually fairly easy to match up (as long as you haven't chosen identical twins as your volunteers!).

6 Thank your volunteers and ask them to return to their seats. If possible, ask a volunteer to stick up the 'portraits' where the students can see them as you speak.

REFLECTION

1 Explain that the Bible says that we have all been made 'in the image of God'. You could read Genesis 1:27 at this point.

2 Explain that this doesn't mean that we are God, or that we look like God, or even that God looks like us! It means that in some way, as human beings, we reflect some of the characteristics of God, for example: when we love others; when we want things to be fair and just. For Christians, Jesus is the perfect example of showing what God is like (Colossians 1:15).

3 Comment that whilst the pictures that have just been drawn are not true or exact representations of their subjects, we can still make out the likeness and recognise the features that make up the different people. The same is true for how your artists have drawn. Similarly, even though we might be not very good 'images' of what God is like, Christians believe that we can see in the way people behave things which remind us of our Creator, God.

RESPONSE

1 In a time of silence, give students the opportunity to:

- Thank God that we have been made in his image.
- Ask for his help to look out for good things in others that remind us about God.
- Ask for his help in showing his qualities in the way we behave.

2 Conclude by reading some Bible verses which show what God is like (eg Colossians 3:12–14).

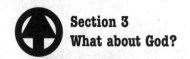

23	**Someone to lean on**

Bible base	Proverbs 3:5
Aim	To help the young people understand that when life gets hard, Christians believe God is there and will help.
Tools needed	❏ A unicycle, or picture of a unicycle (either a large picture or one that can be projected). ❏ Equipment to project unicycle picture (if needed).

PREPARATION

• Locate a unicycle to borrow, or a picture of one.

Note: You could use a child's bike with stabilisers instead of the unicycle; adjust the wording of the outline throughout to be consistent with this.

PRESENTATION

1 Show the unicycle, or picture of one. Ask if anyone in the assembly has ever tried to ride one.

Note: If this happens to be one of your talents, give a brief demonstration at this point, as long as you've checked beforehand that the school is happy for you to do this.

2 Explain how you learn to ride a unicycle. It's best to begin by pushing off from a long wall and trying to centre your weight on the cycle. When you think you are falling you can lean on the wall. But it is only when you put all your weight on the bike that you will stay upright. What happens when the wall runs out? You fall off!

3 Talk about how life can be like that. What is the 'wall' (or other support) they are depending on? What things do they get their sense of security from? What happens when the 'wall' runs out?

4 Give a personal example if possible of a time when everything in your life suddenly went wrong, when everything had seemed just fine. This is how the 'wall' ran out for you. Then tell your story, for example, a day when:

• Your car broke down.
• You had to walk miles in the rain to get help.
• Your mobile phone wasn't charged and ran out of credit.
• Back home, your girlfriend/boyfriend called to say they wanted to break up with you.
• The ceiling fell in.
• Then your goldfish died…

Comment that you felt you had nothing left to lean on. The 'wall' ran out on each of these things. Say that you had a sense of security in them and when everything seemed to be falling apart you got very unhappy. But, because you are a Christian, you knew that God was still there for you and could help you. Ultimately, as a Christian, he is the one you look to for strength and security.

REFLECTION

1 Ask students to think about what they are 'leaning' on? What will happen if the 'wall' (or other support) runs out?

2 Say that depending on God makes sense, at all times, not just in the bad. He doesn't 'run out' – but is always there. Read Proverbs 3:5:

> **'Trust in the Lord with all your heart and
> lean not on your own understanding.'**
>
> Proverbs 3:5 (NIV)

Say that you believe God is utterly reliable and can be trusted totally.

RESPONSE

1 Ask the students to spend a few moments thinking about what things are supporting them in life? What are they depending on? What would happen if those things were taken away?

2 Invite the young people to ask God to help them to 'lean' on him today.

Note: If you do take a unicycle into school, ask about Health and Safety regulations, and check on any concerns there might be about damage to the floor. Don't allow young people to 'try' the cycle.

24 Resolutions

New Year

Bible base	Matthew 28:20; Hebrews 13:8
Aim	To help students reflect on the opportunity the new year brings for a fresh start.
Tools needed	❑ OHP and acetates, or flip chart.

PREPARATION

• Think of a personal – and if possible, amusing and/or entertaining – New Year's resolution anecdote.

• Set up OHP or flip chart before assembly begins.

PRESENTATION

1 Begin by talking about a New Year's resolution you once made – choose one that's not very serious.

2 Ask the students if they have made any New Year's resolutions? If so, what are they? Encourage them to say their serious and not-so-serious ones. As they do, write some up on an OHP acetate or flip chart (eg stop biting finger nails, be nice to their little sister).

3 After you have gathered a few, ask:

• Why do people make resolutions?
• What would help you keep your resolutions?
• What makes it difficult?

Talk about the reasons why people find it hard to keep their resolutions.

4 Ask students to think back to last term. What was good about it? What didn't go so well? Now ask them to think about this term. What are they looking forward to? What are they determined to do better?

5 Now ask them to think about the world. If they could make some New Year's resolutions for the world what would they be? From all their suggestions, what would be their top three for the world. Write these up on the acetate or flip chart. Then ask if they think these 'resolutions' are likely to be kept.

REFLECTION

1 In a time of quiet, ask students to think about the coming year:

· How they would like their own lives to be this year?
· What would they wish for the world?

2 Comment that, whether or not they keep their resolutions, and whatever happens in the world, there are probably going to be some problems and times when they will find things difficult.

3 Say that you are going to read some words from the Bible. Read Hebrews 13:8:

> **'Jesus Christ is the same yesterday, today, and for ever.'**
>
> Hebrews 13:8 (NCV)

Then read the second half of Matthew 28:20, explaining that these are words Jesus said to his followers when he was on earth:

'... I will be with you always, even until the end of this age.'

Matthew 28:20 (NCV)

4 Remind the students that God is with them always. In the coming year, he will be with them through all the bad times, and the good ones too.

RESPONSE

Encourage the students to reflect on the following (the Millennium Resolution written by Churches Together in England) and to make it their own prayer if they wish:

**Let there be
respect for the earth,
peace for its people,
love in our lives,
delight in the good,
forgiveness for past wrongs
and from now on, a new start.**

Resolution reproduced with permission from Churches Together in England.

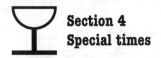
25	**Love, love me do**
	Valentine's Day

Bible base	John 3:16; 1 Corinthians 13:4–13
Aim	To encourage students to think about the meaning of 'true love' and to encourage them to think about how loving they are towards others.
Tools needed	❏ Some Valentine's cards, if possible including some addressed to you. ❏ A modern version of the Bible.

PREPARATION

• Gather some ideas as examples of how love is portrayed in films and adverts (eg James Bond films; the Rolo advert where the person gives away their last Rolo).

• Prepare for the quiz, making sure you have a good number and selection of famous couples currently in the media.

PRESENTATION

Start by telling the students you're going to be thinking about 'love' in this assembly.

Valentine's cards

Ask the students if they have bought any Valentine's Day cards. What are the cards like? What kinds of things will they write on them? Who will they send one to? Why?

Films and adverts

Talk about how 'love' is portrayed in adverts or films (eg James Bond and his many women, the last Rolo chocolate, soaps on TV, Friends). Use some current examples from TV and films. Point out that the way love is portrayed in the media can put pressure on us for how we think our relationships should be. Point out that romantic love is often glamorised. Real life often isn't like the media portrays it.

Famous couples

Introduce this quiz about couples. This could be done with the whole audience participating, or two teams of volunteers at the front, with audience support for each of the teams. The challenge is to name the matching half of these couples when you give one name. For example:

• Richard and (Judy)
• Chandler and (Monica)
• Romeo and (Juliet)
• Brad Pitt and (Jennifer Aniston)
• Marge and (Homer)
• Posh and (Becks)

Use couples who are currently in the media and are likely to be known by the young people. You could use examples from soaps like Neighbours or EastEnders.

Talk about how some of the couples in the quiz have showed their love for one another, for example: Monica and Chandler in Friends were very romantic, with the proposal taking place in a candlelit room; Becks gave Posh an extremely expensive ring and she gave him an expensive sports car; Romeo climbed a balcony for Juliet!

The Bible

Say that the Bible is passionate about love! As an example, read 1 Corinthians 13:4-7. Talk about the kind of love these verses from the Bible are talking about. Say that the Bible also tells us a lot about

God's love for human beings. Read John 3:16. Ask: 'How does this verse tell us God shows his love to us?'

REFLECTION

1 Point out that the kind of love described in the first verses they heard (1 Corinthians 13:4–7) is a description of how Christians believe people should act towards others. These principles can be applied to any of their relationships (eg friends, other students, teachers, parents). Ask students for examples or give some from everyday life (eg an example of not being jealous or envious).

2 Ask the students to think about how loving they really are towards other people. Say you are going to read some of the Bible verses again (1 Corinthians 13:4–7). As they listen, invite them in their imagination to replace the word 'love' with their name, for example, for verse 4: 'Sharon is kind and patient...' Give an example of what you mean, then read the passage slowly and with emphases to prompt students to do this.

3 Ask students if those words really do describe what they are like.

RESPONSE

In a time of quiet:

• ask the students to think about how loving they are towards other people;

• remind them about God's love for them and how he has shown that;

• if they wish, invite them to ask God to help them today to show more kindness and care towards others.

26 All you need is love...

Valentine's Day

Bible base	Matthew 22:39; 1 Corinthians 13:4–13
Aim	To help students think about the meaning of love and about treating others with kindness.
Tools needed	❏ OHP, acetate and pens to write up suggestions from students. ❏ A CD player and CDs with current songs including the word 'love'. ❏ Bible verses from 1 Corinthians 13:4–7 printed onto an OHP acetate or on PowerPoint (optional).

PREPARATION

• Think of four or five current songs which you think students will know which include the word 'love' in the titles or lyrics.

PRESENTATION

1 If possible, play a selection of current songs including the word 'love' as students enter the room where you're meeting for the assembly.

2 Ask students to see how many songs they can come up with which include the word 'love'. You could show them some CD covers as clues. Write the song titles up on an OHP acetate if you have one. How many can they think of?

3 Talk about the fact that love is mentioned a lot in music, in magazines, on TV etc. But what is it? For example, what does it mean to love someone? Ask for some suggestions.

4 Point out that it can mean different things at different times, depending on who you are talking about. Get the students to suggest different people we 'love' (eg boyfriend/girlfriend, Mum, Dad, brother, friends). Comment that the way we love these people is different depending on the kind of relationship we have with them.

5 Say that you're going to read one description of love. Read this passage from the Bible, slowly and thoughtfully: 1 Corinthians 13:4–7. Explain that this is from the Bible and is a description of how Christians believe people should act towards others. These principles can be applied to any of our friendships and relationships. Display the verses now if you wish.

6 Talk through each element of the Bible passage, asking for practical examples of what it might mean to behave like this towards friends, parents, boyfriend/girlfriend, teacher etc.

REFLECTION

1 Invite the students to consider this commandment from the Bible about how we should care for others:

'Love your neighbour as you love yourself.'
Matthew 22:39 (NCV)

2 Comment that this means we should treat people the way we would like to be treated.

RESPONSE

Ask the students to think about their own behaviour and actions. Are there times when they don't 'love' others in the way you've just been talking about? Ask them to think about how they might need to change. Encourage them to ask God to help them to be 'loving' towards others today.

If you wish, you could play a quiet Christian song on the theme of love as students go out from the assembly.

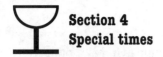
27	# All change!
	Lent

Bible base	Matthew 5:13
Aim	To encourage students to think about what needs to change in their lives.
Tools needed	❑ Salt. ❑ Three bottles of cola (the same brand but different varieties). ❑ Five or six current advert slogans. ❑ Three cups. ❑ Blindfold. ❑ Mars bar (or other chocolate bar).

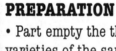

PREPARATION

• Part empty the three bottles of cola. Use three different varieties of the same brand (eg normal, diet cola and lemon). Put a teaspoon of salt in each. (Be careful as the cola will fizz up.) Replace caps, so the bottles are ready for use in the assembly.

PRESENTATION

1 Start with an advert quiz. Read out five or six slogans and get your audience to guess the product. You could do this with you asking everyone to guess, or you could have two teams representing the two halves of your audience. Choose current slogans that the students will be familiar with, for example:

'Because you're worth it.' (L'Oréal)
'Enjoy...' (Coca Cola)
'The devil makes work for idle thumbs.' (Virgin mobile)
'Just do it.' (Nike)
'I'm lovin' it.' (McDonald's)

2 Comment that good adverts are very successful at making a product known. Mention one or two that you remember from when you were a teenager. Then ask:

• If you were the product, what would the advertisers say about you?

Ask them to think about whether they would be happy with what they might say? Would other people get the right message about you?

3 Ask for a volunteer who likes cola. Explain that you've got three different varieties. Say that you want them to see if they can tell the difference. Blindfold them. Pour out some of each variety into the cups and get them to take the taste challenge. Can they can guess the types of cola? You should find that they won't be able to, as the salt will have changed the flavour.

4 Explain that the challenge was difficult because you had, in fact, added some salt to the cola before the assembly. Thank your volunteer and give a small prize (eg a Mars bar), to make up for the salty cola.

REFLECTION

1 Comment that salt changes things. The presence of the salt in the cola had changed it. Read Matthew 5:13.

2 Salt always makes a difference – usually a good difference (think of chips without salt!). Christians believe that, like the words in the Bible we've just heard, Jesus wants us to be like salt to the people we meet, changing things for the better.

3 Explain that it's Lent – the time leading up to Easter, when the death and resurrection of Jesus is remembered. Christians see this as a time to think about their lives and how they need to change (eg any bad habits).

RESPONSE

In a time of quiet, encourage students to think about the things in their lives which need to change.

• Does the way they live change things for the better for others?

• Have they got some bad habits? Wrong attitudes?

Say that Christians believe that God will help us to change, if we ask. If appropriate, pray, asking God to help us to change and be more like Jesus.

28 Pancakes

Lent

Bible base	Mark 8:31–38
Aim	To help students think about the meaning of Lent.
Tools needed	❏ Two or three pancakes – made slightly thicker than usual. ❏ A frying pan.

PREPARATION

• Prepare your pancakes! You may only need one – the others are spares in case the first one gets broken.

PRESENTATION

1 Ask the students what they think is special about this time of year. Help them, if necessary, towards the answer: Pancake Day!

2 Show the frying pan with one of the (cold) pancakes already in it. Ask if anyone is good at flipping pancakes. Ask for a couple of volunteers and let them try. Encourage applause for the best effort and let your volunteers sit down.

3 Now ask the students if they know the reason for Pancake Day. Encourage some answers, then briefly talk about their responses.

4 Talk about Lent, explaining that it is the time leading up to Easter. Jesus spent 40 days fasting (going without food) in the desert, thinking and praying about what God had sent him to do.

5 Explain the reason for Pancake Day. Some Christians believe that they should give up foods, as a way of showing that they are remembering Jesus' time in the desert, spending more time praying and fasting as Jesus did. In order to clear out food from their store cupboards, people used to make pancakes. Then, during the time of Lent, they wouldn't eat any rich foods. This tradition led to us having pancakes on Shrove Tuesday. Ask whether any of the students are intending to give up something for Lent (eg chocolate).

6 Show the pancake to the students again. Holding it up, talk about what a wonderful thing a pancake is – it can be used for all kinds of things! Give some silly examples, acting them out as you say them, for example: 'You could use it to shine your shoes; as a face cloth; to wash under your armpits; as a hat; to play Frisbee.' Then say, 'Or, you could eat it.' Begin to eat it! You could pretend to offer it to some of your audience as well!

REFLECTION

1 Put the pancake to one side. Then talk briefly about Easter. Explain that at the first Easter time, just over 2,000 years ago, Jesus died a horrible death on a cross. He gave up his life. Christians believe that he gave up all he had in heaven to come to earth for us.

2 Lent is a good opportunity to take some time, like Jesus did, to think about what God wants us to do with our lives. Or, to consider if there is anything in our lives which we think God would want us to give up.

3 At this point, you may wish to read Mark 8:31,34–36. Explain that these are some words from the Bible about Jesus when he was talking about his death.

RESPONSE

1 In a short time of silence, invite the students:

• to take a moment to think about how they would feel if they had to give up something very precious to them. Ask them to reflect on how Jesus gave up his life for us.

• to think about what God might want them to do with their lives.

• to think whether there are things in their lives – apart from chocolate – which aren't right? Encourage students to make a decision to change, asking God's help to do so, if they'd like to.

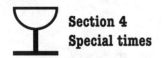

29	**Egg race**
	Easter

Bible base	John 11:25,26
Aim	To help students learn more about the meaning of Easter.
Tools needed	❏ Three Cadbury's Creme Eggs (or similar).
	❏ An advert for Cadbury's Creme Eggs (or similar).
	❏ A stopwatch.
	❏ Mini chocolate eggs – enough for one for everyone in the assembly (optional, depending on school and your finances!).

PREPARATION

• Find out, if possible, the current 'world record' for time taken to eat a Cadbury's Creme Egg, or have a suitable other 'record' ready (eg from other schools, youth groups etc visited).

PRESENTATION

1 Ask the students some questions about Easter eggs, eg:

• Who likes chocolate?
• How many Easter eggs did you get last year?

2 Show an advert for Creme Eggs. Show them a Cadbury's Creme Egg – hinting that someone in this assembly might get the egg!

3 Tell them the 'record' time taken to eat a Creme Egg. Ask if anyone thinks they could beat that.

4 Ask for two volunteers (who like Creme Eggs!). Give them both a Creme Egg and challenge them to see who can eat their egg in the shorter time. Will either of them beat the record?

Use a stop-watch for timing. Make sure that both competitors start at the same time, on your 'Go!'. Encourage support for both (making sure that both volunteers have support!). You could ask half the audience to support one competitor, and one part the other one. Build up the atmosphere by commentating as the contest develops.

Cheer the winner. Announce the times. Is there a new record? Award the winner another egg as their prize.

 REFLECTION

1 Comment that it's great getting – and eating – Easter eggs at Easter, but what's the point of them? Ask the students to suggest some answers.

2 Respond to answers given by students. These might include:

• New life
• Baby chicks being born
• Spring/new life beginning
• Jesus coming back to life

3 Talk briefly about the answers you receive, making sure that the above are included. Then go on to explain that Christians believe Jesus' death and resurrection – his coming back to life – mean that forgiveness, new life and the chance to start again are possible for everyone.

RESPONSE

1 In a time of quiet, ask students to think about:

• What does Easter mean to me?
• Are there any ways in which I need to make a new start?

2 Pray, if appropriate, then wish everyone 'Happy Easter'!

Optional extra: Tell students that you're going to give them each a mini-Easter egg as they leave. As they eat it, ask them to think about anything they need forgiveness for, or ways in which they need to make a fresh start. Say that they could even ask God to help them with that. (Make sure you encourage them to put the wrapping in a rubbish bin!)

30	**Light and dark**
	Halloween

Bible base	Matthew 15:16–20; Luke 11:33–36; John 1:4,5; 9:5
Aim	To help students reflect on what causes evil and Jesus' reassurance that he is the light of the world.
Tools needed	❏ Appropriate pictures from newspapers etc to remind students of 'evil' events that are currently in the news (bombings, crimes which have hurt people, oppression) – these could be prepared for display on PowerPoint or OHP acetates.
	❏ A candle and matches (optional).
	❏ Flip chart and pens (optional).

PREPARATION

• Search out and prepare for display pictures you plan to use.

Note: When you refer to Halloween, take care not to appear to trivialise it or associated topics, which may be frightening issues for some students (eg the occult and supernatural).

PRESENTATION

1 Start by talking briefly about Halloween. Point out how, although most people don't take Halloween seriously, there is real evil in the world which is very serious. Ask the students for some examples of 'evil' they've noticed recently in the news.

2 Show them some of the pictures you've selected as reminders of 'evil' that's happened recently and talk about the kinds of 'evil' these represent.

3 Ask:

• Why did these bad things happen?
• Who was responsible?

4 Say that while we would probably never do some of the terrible things they've just looked at, all of us do sometimes do 'evil' things. Asking students for their ideas, make a list (on OHP or flip chart) of different 'evil' things they might do (eg bullying, telling lies, taking something which isn't theirs). Even though these aren't big crimes, they are still small steps in the wrong direction and often result in hurt for others.

REFLECTION
1 Dark

Comment that most of the evil and suffering in the world is caused by human beings. The Bible talks about the wrong things we do coming from within us. It's our own fault! Christians believe that God created human beings with the ability to choose right from wrong: a lot of the time evil is caused by people who deliberately choose wrong.

2 Light

Christians believe that the power of evil has been overcome through the death of Jesus on the cross. If we do wrong things, God will forgive us when we say sorry to him, and will help us to do what's right.

RESPONSE

1 Light a candle, placed so that people can see it. Then read out Jesus' words, saying:

'Jesus said, "I am the light of the world."'

John 9:5 (NIV)

2 Ask students to consider:

• Have you contributed towards evil in any ways?
• What good have you done recently?

3 Invite students, if they wish, to take a moment as everyone is quiet to ask God to forgive them for wrong things they've done and to find ways of bringing some 'light' into others' lives today.

4 Conclude by reading John 1:4,5, explaining that these are some words from the Bible about Jesus.

Note: Check that the school's Health and Safety rules will allow you to light a candle during assembly.

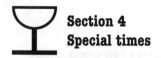

31 I remember when

Remembrance

Bible base	Matthew 5:9,38–48
Aim	To help students think about the importance of forgiveness and seeking to make peace, and the importance of remembering.
Tools needed	❏ Items from the past, eg old vinyl records, Rubik's Cube, large mobile phone, recordings of old songs to play.
	❏ Items from their lives today, eg current CDs, the latest games console, small mobile phone.
	❏ Equipment to play old songs, if using.
	❏ Remembrance Day poppies.
	❏ OHP and acetate (optional).

PREPARATION

• Set up equipment for playing music, if using.

• Devise extra quiz questions, if needed.

• If you have enough poppies to give the students one each, get some volunteers to give them out as the students enter.

• If using, prepare the words from the Kohima Memorial on an OHP acetate.

PRESENTATION

1 Show the students some of the items from the past you've brought in. You might like even to play an old song or two. Talk about how the items from the past have been surpassed by newer things.

2 Do this quiz, encouraging participation: 'I remember when...' The students have to tell you the year of the events. Below are some memorable events and their dates. Depending on time you have available, you might want to add some more notable dates.

You could do the quiz either by simply asking the audience, with hands up for answers; by dividing the audience in two, each section competing against each other; or having a competition between two teams of volunteers at the front.

Ask: 'In which year did the following events take place?'

• JF Kennedy shot (1963)
• Man landed on the moon (1969)
• The Falklands war (1982)
• Bomb at the Atlanta Olympics (1996)
• Princess Diana died (1997)
• The World Trade Center destroyed by terrorist attack (2001)

3 Talk about the idea of history repeating itself, for example:

• Old fashions come back into fashion, eg mini-skirts, flares.
• War reoccurs, eg Falklands War, Gulf War, Northern Ireland, Kosovo, Afghanistan, Iraq.
• Violence and terrorism, eg September 11, suicide bombs in Israel.

4 Show the students a Remembrance Day poppy. Explain that these were first sold and worn as reminders of the fields of France covered in red poppies during World War I and also reminders of the bloodshed in wars since.

After the two major world wars in Europe in the first half of the last century, the British Legion wanted future generations never to forget the atrocities of war and to remember those who had died for their country.

5 Say that they might have heard these words, often spoken at this time of year, in remembrance of people who have given their lives in wars (display these words on an OHP, if using):

> **'They shall grow not old as we who are left grow old, age shall not weary them nor the years condemn. At the going down of the sun and in the morning we will remember them. When you go home, tell them of us and say, "For your tomorrow we gave our today."'**
>
> Kohima Memorial in Burma

6 Explain that some Christians, who were pacifists, did not fight in the two World Wars, believing that, whatever the reasons, it is always wrong to kill others and that other ways of making peace should be found. Other Christians believed it was right to go to war and gave their lives to preserve freedom and peace for others.

7 Explain that, whether we believe war is right or wrong, the Bible talks about the importance of being willing to forgive, and about reconciliation and seeking peace wherever possible. That applies to every day quarrels between people too.

8 Read out some of these verse from the Bible: Matthew 5:9,38–48.

REFLECTION

Ask the students:

• How would you like to be remembered?
• In what ways could you contribute to making peace (in school, your family, your community, the world)?
• Can you forgive others, when you need to, and not seek revenge or retribution?

RESPONSE

1 Tell the students you are going to have a short time of quiet, when you want them to think honestly about the following:

• Are there people at home or school who they need to forgive?

Tell them they could ask God to help them forgive others.

• How could they help make peace between themselves and someone else, or even in the wider world?

Remind them they could ask God to help them do something about this today.

2 Finally, get them to look at their own poppy or the one you're showing them. Encourage them, every time they see one of these at this time of year, to remember what it means and to let it challenge them to work for peace, in big and small ways.

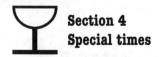

Section 4
Special times

32	A time to remember
	Remembrance

Bible base	1 Corinthians 11:23–26
Aim	To help students reflect on how memories are an important part of our lives.
Tools needed	❏ A recording of 'Everything I do, I do it for you' by Bryan Adams.
	❏ PowerPoint equipment (optional) or OHP and acetates for presentation.
	❏ Objects, photos etc that you plan to use as examples in the assembly.
	❏ Remembrance Day poppies.

PREPARATION

• Find the pictures or objects you plan to use in the assembly.

• Find out some facts about wars by doing a web search.

• If using PowerPoint or OHP for presentation of pictures (see below), prepare material as appropriate.

• Wear a poppy.

PRESENTATION

1 Start by talking about the different ways in which we remember things, pointing out that we have good memories and sad memories. Show some examples, beginning with some personal ones. You could show some of your 'picture' memories using PowerPoint or OHP and also some actual objects, holding them up for your audience to see. Choose things which you think this age group will enjoy. Examples might include:

Good memories

• Photographs (eg a funny one of you on holiday as a child)
• Your teddy bear
• Your diary – includes important dates (eg your birthday, pay day, holidays, trip to the cinema)

Sad memories

• Possessions (eg your grandma's wedding ring)
• Photographs (eg a picture of a relative who fought/died in a war)

2 Now comment that some students are wearing poppies (if they are). Show and talk about your Remembrance Day poppy. Ask if anyone can tell you why we wear these at this time of year. Then talk about what the poppy is meant to help us remember. Include some facts about wars, for example:

On the first day of the Battle of the Somme in WWI, there were nearly 60,000 casualties, a third of whom were killed.

Talk about the fact that the people who were killed or injured were real people – someone's father, brother, husband or son. In the First World War, some of those fighting were very young – as young as 14.

3 Ask: 'Why is it important to remember?'

• Talk about a time you forgot something (eg your Mum's birthday!). How did that make the person feel?
• Talk about the importance of remembering friends and relatives who have died, including some personal examples. If we don't remember people it's as if we're saying they weren't important or that we don't care about the contribution they've made to our lives.

In the same way, it's important to remember the people who have died in wars, fighting for things that are important. How we live today is partly due to their sacrifice. Remembrance Day is a time to remember.

REFLECTION

1 Say that remembering is important, as what happened in the past affects our lives now. It's important because others (those we don't know, like soldiers, and those we do know, like family) have done things for us which have an effect on our lives today and we need to remember them with thankfulness.

2 Now show the cross (an object, or picture on OHP or PowerPoint). Talk about how for Christians it's important to remember how Jesus died and in doing so took all the suffering and wrongs of the world. When we see a cross it reminds us of Jesus giving up his life for us, and challenges us about how we live for God and others now.

RESPONSE

1 Ask the young people to think about:

• the soldiers who gave their lives for this country;
• good memories of people and what they mean to them;
• Jesus giving up his life on the cross and why he did that.

Give a few moments of silence and encourage students to take the time to say thank you to God for what these memories mean and to think about what difference they might make to their lives now.

2 Show the prepared PowerPoint presentation (optional) with images of memories (family photos, war pictures), ending with one showing the cross, whilst listening to the song you have selected on the theme of remembering.

If PowerPoint isn't available, use two or three OHP acetates with images and display these whilst the students are listening to the song.

3 End with a time of silence, leaving the image of the cross on display.

33 Get ready!

Advent

Bible base	Matthew 2:1–12
Aim	To encourage students to think about why we celebrate Christmas.
Tools needed	❑ Two boxes.
	❑ Sheets of Christmas wrapping paper, pre-cut if necessary, ready to wrap the boxes.
	❑ Two rolls of sticky tape.
	❑ Eight envelopes.
	❑ Eight cards.
	❑ Two address lists (four addresses on each).
	❑ Eight mince pies.
	❑ Two sets of words of a carol.
	❑ Four Christmas chocolates as prizes.
	❑ Three more boxes, one wrapped in gold and the two others in plain colours, labelled with large letters: 'gold', 'frankincense' and 'myrrh'.

PREPARATION

• Before the assembly begins, set up a table with all the items necessary in place for the team game. As far as possible, make sure that the table is arranged so that the audience can see the teams' efforts.

• Place the three gifts of the Wise Men separately to avoid them getting spoilt in the team game. These could be put on view to act as a focus through the assembly.

PRESENTATION

1 Start by talking about getting ready for Christmas and students' preparations. Ask for eight volunteers to take part in the team game.

Note: Check for food allergies.

2 Have two teams of four people in each. Explain that both teams have to complete four activities to do with getting ready for Christmas. The activities are:

• Wrap up a 'gift'.
• Write four cards and put each in its envelope which must be addressed.
• Eat four mince pies.
• Sing a carol.

Involve the audience by having one half supporting Team A and the others supporting Team B. Give prizes to the winning team and encourage applause for all the volunteers.

3 When everyone is quiet again, comment that this time of year coming up to Christmas is called Advent. It's the time when Christians get ready for Christmas – not just wrapping presents and writing cards – but by thinking about the reason for Christmas.

If appropriate to your audience, ask them what they think are reasons for Christmas (eg presents, parties etc). Say that, really, it's a celebration of the birth of Jesus.

4 Talk about the story of the Wise Men. Ask the students if they can remember what gifts they brought to Jesus. Explain that each of their gifts tells us something about who Jesus is and what he had come to do.

5 Now show the audience each of your ready-prepared, labelled gifts.

Gold

Say that gold was thought of as a gift for a king. Christians believe that Jesus is King – God's Son – and his special gift to us.

Frankincense

Explain that this was a substance with a strong smell which was used by priests, like incense. A priest was someone who talked to God on behalf of the people. Christians believe that Jesus, a bit like a priest, came to help us know God and show us what he is like.

Myrrh

Myrrh was a substance that was used to cover bodies before they were buried. Explain that Christians believe that this gift reminds us about Jesus' death for us – so that we could be put right with God.

REFLECTION

Encourage the students, as they get ready for Christmas this year, to take some time to think about these questions:

• Where is Jesus in your Christmas?
• How could you and your family include him in the festivities which started because of his birth?

RESPONSE

In a time of quiet, encourage students to pray, or lead with a short prayer yourself, using this or similar outline:

• Thanks for Christmas and fun: what do they especially enjoy about Christmas?

• Thanks for Jesus: ask them to think about the three gifts of the Wise Men and what those tell us about Jesus. Give thanks for his coming to earth for us.

• Ask God's help to remember Jesus this Christmas.

Note: Check first with the school that it is OK for you to offer mince pies to students and that this isn't a problem regarding possible food allergies.

34 Gifts

Christmas

Bible base	Matthew 2:11; John 3:16
Aim	To encourage students to remember that the reason for Christmas and presents is to celebrate the birthday of Jesus, God's gift to the world.
Tools needed	❏ Party hat, large birthday badge (eg '18 today').
	❏ Five or six 'presents', eg small bags of sweets (optional, see 'Note').
	❏ A CD which the age group would enjoy for a party.
	❏ A bag of crisps.
	❏ A can of drink.
	❏ A CD of the carol you plan to use.
	❏ Equipment to play the CD.

PREPARATION

• Before the assembly, wrap up the 'presents'.

• Set up equipment for playing the CD in the assembly, and make sure it all works.

• 'Party guest' volunteers. Before the assembly, enlist the help of four or five volunteers and give them one of the 'presents'. Explain briefly that you are going to ask them to the front, bringing their 'present' with them, and then to act as if they are enjoying a party. You will tell them what to do as the assembly progresses. You might like to ask the teacher responsible for the assembly to select 'appropriate' volunteers for you. See 'Note' at the end of the outline (optional).

PRESENTATION

1 Start by talking about parties.

• Are they going to any parties this Christmas?
• Have they been to/had any good birthday parties?

2 Say that you want them to imagine how they would feel if the following happened at their birthday party. (Put on a party hat yourself, badge with '18 today' etc at this point.)

Say that:

You are going to have a party. You invite your friends and they are all going to come. The food and drink look great.

(Bring out a token bag of crisps and can of drink!)

It's all ready. Everyone comes.

(At this point, invite your 'party guest' volunteers to come to the front carrying their presents. Put on the CD, keeping volume low, so you can be heard. Encourage your volunteers to act as if they are at a party.)

Say that all is going well. You notice that they've each brought a present with them – and you think, 'Great – wonder what I've got!'

Then the music stops.

(Turn off the music.)

People start getting out their presents.

(Encourage your 'party guests' to look at their presents.)

You wait for them to give you the presents – after all, it is your birthday.

(Look excited.)

But they don't. Your friends give each other the presents!

(Encourage your 'party guests' to give one another the presents and to unwrap them, dropping the paper on the floor, leaving you out.)

Ask, 'How would you feel if this was your party?'

(Thank your volunteers and ask them to go back to their places.)

Say that the party is over. All your friends have gone and you have been left on your own with just the wrappings.

REFLECTION

1 Say that maybe that's how Jesus feels about Christmas. Briefly comment on how there's lots of partying at Christmas. Then ask about the meaning of Christmas, 'Whose birthday is it anyway?'

2 Talk about how today we often forget that Christmas is about celebrating Jesus' birthday. We get preoccupied with thinking about the presents we're going to give to other people, and what we're going to get. This is a contrast to the first Christmas when Jesus was the centre of attention and three very special gifts were given to the baby. Briefly explain that gold was for a king, frankincense for a priest and myrrh, used in burial customs, reminds us of Jesus' death.

3 Explain that Christians started giving gifts to each other at Christmas as a reminder and celebration of God's gift of Jesus to the world. At this point, you could read from the Bible: John 3:16.

RESPONSE

1 In a time of quiet:

• Ask the students to think about the presents they plan to give, and the ones they hope to get. Encourage them to let every present, this Christmas, be a reminder of how God showed his love for us through his gift of Jesus to the world.

• Thank God for sending Jesus into the world for us.

• Ask the students if they can think of someone who is going to be left out of Christmas celebrations this year. Is there something they could do, or a gift they could give, to show them some of God's love – just as God did for us when he sent Jesus.

2 You could finish the time of quiet by listening to a verse from a Christmas carol about God's gift of Jesus at Christmas (eg the appropriates verse from 'O Little Town of Bethlehem', 'The First Nowell' or 'We Three Kings'). Alternatively, you could read the words.

Wish everyone a very happy Christmas!

Note: If you don't wish to involve volunteers or it's not easy to do so, simply use the outline as above, omitting the sections about inviting volunteers to the front and instructions to them as you talk about the party. You can still set the scene by putting on the hat and badge yourself, playing the CD etc.